The Ultimate Breakthrough in Market Turning Point Detection

Catching Every Major Pivot in Stocks, Options and Futures with the PAMA Method

Jeffrey A. Cuddy

©1997 by Jeffrey A. Cuddy

Published by Windsor Books
P.O. Box 280
Brightwaters, NY 11718

Editing, internal design and composition, and cover design by:
Professional Resources & Communications, Inc.

Printed in the United States of America

ISBN 0-930233-61-1

Dedication

To Min,
my wife and my love

Acknowledgments

I was indeed most fortunate to have Jeff Schmidt, managing editor of Windsor Books, guide me through the completion of this book. If it were not for his encouragement and expertise, the task would not have been possible.

Also, a special thanks to Janet Potter of Professional Resources & Communications, Inc., who so skillfully smoothed over the rough edges of the text, and to Theresa Fenske, who designed many of the graphs and laid out the book.

Contents

Introduction

The Ultimate Breakthrough in Market Turning Point Detection introduces a new dimension in technical analysis. In the pages that follow, I will present an exciting way to profit in all freely traded markets—stocks, mutual funds and, most important of all, the futures markets, where huge profits can be captured trading diverse commodities such as soybeans, pork bellies and silver, among others.

This method does not require a computer or complicated mathematics. Most importantly, the method works—quickly, easily and with astounding accuracy.

My formulation of this system started during the great bear market of 1973–1974 in which markets lost more than half their value. I experienced severe losses by entering and leaving the market at the wrong time, the victim of damaging whipsaws. From this experience came a strong desire to understand the inner workings of the market—not only for my own benefit, but perhaps, for the benefits of others who might otherwise be caught in a similar trap.

Despite the uncertain and as yet unproved value of technical analysis, my own evaluations of various systems led me to believe that it is possible to tilt the odds in your favor over random market behavior. However, none of the systems that I had come across impressed me well enough to use in actual trading.

After several years of tinkering and experimenting, the **PAMA Method**, emerged as an original trading approach capable of calling the highs and lows of virtually all freely traded markets. Although the system started with the study of the stock market, I discovered that the commodity markets held far greater profit potential. The rules of operation are quite similar for both markets. Right now I would like to preview those rules—and the **PAMA Method** as a whole—before presenting a more in-depth discussion in Section I.

The purpose of the **PAMA Method** is to identify the tops and bottoms of market cycles, in order to buy near the lows and sell near the highs. And note here that when I use the phrase "market cycles" I am not referring to seasonal or strictly calendar-based cyclical moves, but rather to the constant ebb and flow in price pulsing through every freely traded market—the natural rhythms and undulating nature of price that creates volatility and profit opportunities.

With **PAMA**, most market cycles are identified by constant-width channels that alternate up and down at a 45-degree angle, with a pivotal area in between—the pivotal area being the crucial transition zone through which price travels as it changes channels. In fact, that crucial transition zone is from where **PAMA** derives its name—the ***Pivotal Area of Market Analysis***. Fact is, if you can interpret this area correctly, you can indeed buy low and sell high.

PAMA begins with a simple, time-related equation that underlies most pivotal areas, namely, **1 + 2 = 3 + 4**. Although confusing to understand at first, and clearly mathematically incorrect, this "equation" actually represents a price relationship that becomes quite simple and easy to work with as you follow it through its various forms in Section I. This relationship, also presented in the form **1, 2 = 3, 4**, is often hidden on charts, but at times can be quite obvious. It refers to the number of days between two highs (1, 2) equaling the number of days between lows (3, 4). **PAMA** uses this guiding principle to find the last day at the bottom of a cycle—the perfect place to buy. Conversely, naturally, it also finds the last day at the top of a cycle—the perfect place to sell.

Of course, this underlying principle of monitoring time between extreme points to forecast turns rarely manifests itself in a neat and perfectly ordered fashion. More often than not, the equation is usually hidden and must be ferreted out from the market action. That's accomplished using deviations, which are simply technical adjustments that align actual market action with the perfect **1, 2 = 3, 4** equation. Making deviation adjustments actually involves bringing smaller cycles into play in order to satisfy the larger **1, 2 = 3, 4** equation.

Please keep in mind that all these concepts will become much clearer in the pages to follow. I'm just previewing **PAMA** here, laying the groundwork for the more in-depth presentation to come.

PAMA's next step involves factoring in elements of ***support and resistance*** (for our purposes, support and resistance refer to the trail of lows and highs from recent market activity). As you are probably aware, support and resistance zones often stop falling prices or stall further advances. **PAMA** uses something called ***extensions*** to incorporate these very important and very real barrier zones into its analysis. Extensions simply shift the time element to a longer or shorter **1, 2 = 3, 4** equation, which will, in some instances, change the ***target day*** (the expected turn day).

A final technique incorporated into **PAMA** is something called the **T**. Its function is to act as a back-up and confirmer of the target day. As I'll soon show you, the arms of the **T** stretch from the top of one cycle to the top of an adjoining cycle, with the upright stem of the **T** wedged in between. The right arm of the **T** points to the day that prices may reverse.

When all is said and done, once you've mastered these basic **PAMA** trading techniques, you'll have at your disposal (for life!) a method that uses channels—and particularly transition zones between channels—to distinguish actual meaningful high and low price turning points from false reversals that "don't take hold." Diligent application of the concepts presented herein will provide you with all the profit-making advantages of *The Ultimate Breakthrough in Market Turning Point Detection*.

And remember as you progress through *Section I*, please be patient until all concepts have been presented. To really grasp the method in its entirety, you must work with it a little, and allow the ideas time to sink in. Then you will be in a position to understand *Section II*, which traces the Dow Jones Industrial Averages from 1987–1995. The study there starts with $10,000 in January 1987 and ends in March 1995 with $40,685—nearly doubling a buy and hold strategy.

Section III turns the spotlight on the futures market where profits are staggering. This section starts with specialized rules for commodities, necessitated by the enormous leverage these markets have to offer. The following futures, picked at random and tracked from 5/18/93 to 8/22/95, are analyzed with instructive walk-through examples:

Commodity	Profit	Loss	Net	No. Trades	% Profitable Trades
S&P 500	60125	4000	+ 56125	10	80%
Pork Bellies	18504	4760	+ 13744	15	67%
Silver	16150	1850	+ 14300	13	77%
Soybeans	9050	2000	+ 7050	10	70%
Swiss Franc	48097	5675	+ 42422	17	71%

Whether you trade in the futures market or the stock market, it is my sincere hope that you will realize greater profits and satisfaction using the **PAMA Method** than you ever thought possible.

Section I

The PAMA Method:
Rules and Analysis

◆◆◆◆

Getting Started

The Pivotal Area

Tips and Procedures

Getting Started

To apply the **PAMA Method**, you will construct a unique chart of your own. Using data obtained daily from the markets, you will maintain this chart on an ongoing basis. To construct this specialized chart, you need some basic supplies.

Supplies

First, you need graph paper. In the Dow Jones studies, the graph paper has 88 squares vertically and 116 squares horizontally. Although the actual number of squares is not critical, try to find blue-lined paper with at least 80 squares vertically (it can be found in many stationery and art stores). You will also need a loose-leaf notebook, ballpoint pen, well-sharpened pencil or fineline eversharp pencil, and a daily newspaper.

Prices and Days

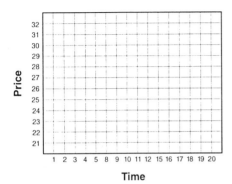

Figure 1

In Figure 1, the figures on the left side of the graph represent prices, while the figures on the bottom represent market days. Weekends and market holidays are ignored. Note that day 5 skips to day 8, and day 12 to day 15.

How To Establish the Price Scale

An important feature of the **PAMA Method** is to establish the proper price scale for each stock, mutual fund or commodity that you are following. All figures must occupy about the same number of squares on the graph paper. For example, if the Dow Jones Industrial Average is priced at 3800 and the S&P 500 is priced at only 450, you must find a way for both to appear to have about the same price range.

To arrive at the price scale, use the following formula:

1. Find the high and low prices over the past 52 weeks. This information is found in various publications (e.g., *Wall Street Journal, Barron's*).

2. Divide 35 into the price range. For example, in 1994 the Dow had a range of 385 points. Divide 385 by 35; the quotient is 11; round to 10. The S&P had a range of only 43 points. Divide 43 by 35; the quotient is 1.2; round to 1 point per square.

The way this would appear on a graph is illustrated in Figure 2.

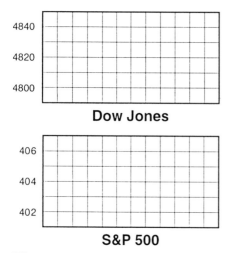

Dow Jones

S&P 500

Figure 2

When figuring the scale, disregard decimal points. For example, if the Dow had been a mutual fund with a price of 38.40, treat it as if it were 3840.

In past years, the Dow has been kept on a scale of 10 points per square, and the S&P 500 on a scale of 1 point per square. Even though the Dow doubled in price between 1987 and 1995, this has worked quite well.

For some issues, high volatility can take place within a relatively small yearly range, and vice versa. For that reason, the formula for establishing a scale can only be a starting point.

Charts and Their Prices

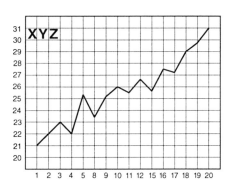

Figure 3

The first step is to connect each day's closing with the previous day's closing until you see a pattern develop (see Figure 3). Starting with the first day, XYZ closed at 21. The next day, it closed up one point to 22. The third day, it went up to 23. The fourth day, XYZ dropped to 22, etc.

Channels and Their Construction

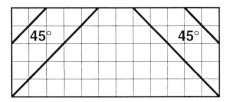

Figure 4

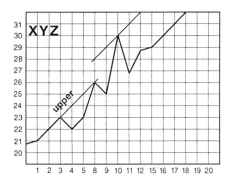

Figure 5

The next step is to organize the patterns as they occur. This is accomplished by drawing **channels**. All channels are drawn at a 45-degree angle—they either rise at a 45-degree angle or fall at a 45-degree angle. This is accomplished by drawing a diagonal from one corner of a square to the other (see Figures 4 and 5).

Every channel contains an upper and lower channel line. First, consider the upper channel line; it touches the highest price before retracing. In Figure 5, notice that, on the third day, XYZ went to 23 before retracing to 22. On the eighth day, XYZ went to 26, touching the upper channel line. On the tenth day, a new upper channel line was drawn because XYZ jumped to 30 before retracing.

The lower channel line is constructed so that it will always be parallel to the upper channel line. Pick a spot somewhere on the upper channel line and count 8 1/2 squares to the right, and place a dot. Next, draw a 45-degree angle from there, thus making a channel with parallel lines (see Figure 6).

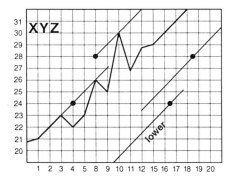

Figure 6

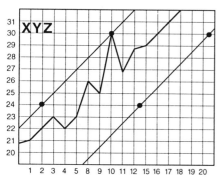

Figure 7

The next step is to simplify the channels. Erase all but the highest channel lines. Note: Remember to draw channel lines with a well-sharpened pencil and to note prices in ink (see Figure 7).

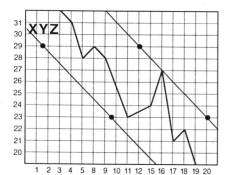

Figure 8

A descending channel has the same construction as the ascending channel (see Figure 8). Note: The relationship between the channel width and the 52-week price range has been calculated carefully. ***Do not try to change the channel width.***

Up-Channels and Down-Channels

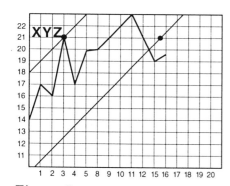

Figure 9

Figure 9 shows that the price of XYZ has violated the ascending channel. That is, it has gone through the lower channel line on the fifteenth day at 19. The next market day—the sixteenth—it rose to 19 1/2.

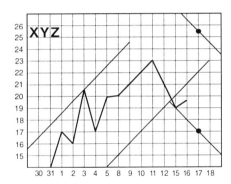

Figure 10

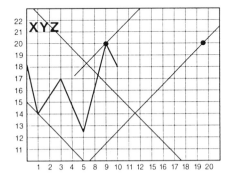

Figure 11

On the *first day* that the channel has been violated (see Figure 10):

1. Draw a downline at 45 degrees from the closing price.

2. Anywhere on that line, count 8 1/2 squares up and place a dot.

3. From that dot, draw a downline 45 degrees parallel to the lower line to form a channel.

Figure 11 illustrates the reverse of Figure 10. A high has been formed outside the descending channel. Construct an ascending channel using the high at 20 on the ninth day for the upper channel line. Then draw in the lower channel line.

The purpose of channels is to identify the primary trend of the market—either it is going up or down. There are no sideways channels.

To save time and effort constructing channels, cut a thin piece of good quality plastic or cardboard 6 inches long. Find the width by measuring 8 1/2 squares on whatever size graph paper you are using. I use a clear plastic guide exactly 6 inches × 1/2 inch and 1/6 inch thick. (See page 149 for a special offer.)

The Pivotal Area

The **PAMA Method** is a breakthrough in detecting the transition from an upmarket to a downmarket, and vice versa. Thoroughly knowing this pivotal area, with the use of channels, can mean the difference between a profit or a loss in the daily bullish/bearish tug-of-war. However, this does not imply that every change in channel direction constitutes a buy or sell signal; it simply means that the balance has tilted in favor of either a bullish or bearish mode. *What does constitute a buy/sell signal is found locked inside this transition from one channel direction to the next.*

Figure 12 illustrates the pivotal areas between market cycles. Notice the flattening out process that takes place before prices change direction. The **PAMA Method** does a remarkable job of distinguishing between false breakouts and the real thing.

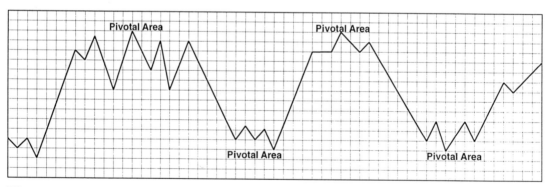

Figure 12

Within the pivotal area, three significant factors have been isolated to point to the probable direction of the market:

1. Target day

2. Support and resistance

3. The *"T"*

Each of these factors will be described in detail. Then they will be blended together to form a meaningful signal.

Target Day and Its Construction

It is not enough just to buy into a strong market trend (as seen in Figure 12) because much of the profits will evaporate as you try to guess if the trend has really started. You want to take a position well within the trading range when the bulls and bears are still battling it out.

Particularly in the pivotal area, the up-and-down gyrations of the market are often seen as well-balanced phenomenon when the number of updays more or less equal the downdays. Visualize a bull market suddenly stalling and going sideways: For three days, the market may go down followed by three days when the market may go up, only to fall again for three more days. How this information can be used to forecast market action will be shown in the figures to follow.

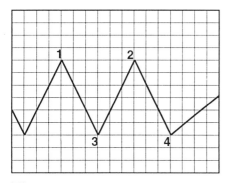

Figure 13

An equation can be stated for Figure 13 as follows:

1, 2 = 3, 4   or

1, 3 = 2, 4

To clarify this, count the number of squares horizontally. For example, between points **1** and **2** there are six days, and between points **1** and **3** there are three days.

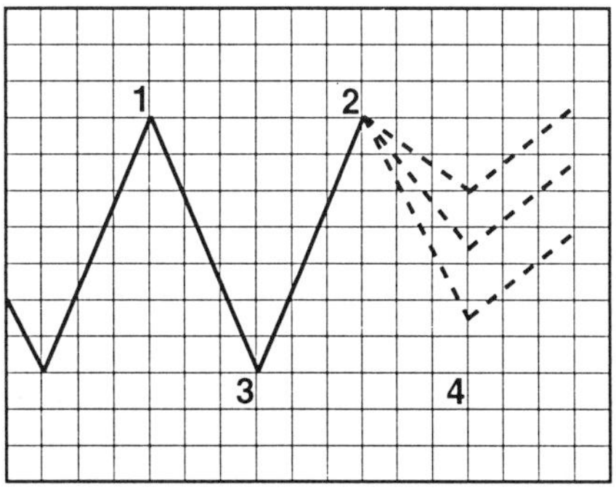

In Figure 14, if points **1, 2** and **3** are known, then it is easy to locate point **4**, which is *target day.*

Target day (point 4) is the day in which prices may reverse their direction. As far as the price level of point **4** is concerned, it could fall anywhere as shown by the dotted line.

Figure 14

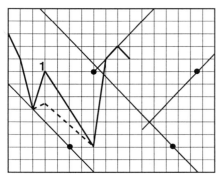

Figure 15

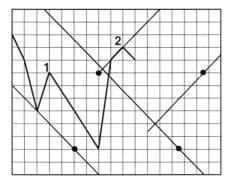

Figure 16

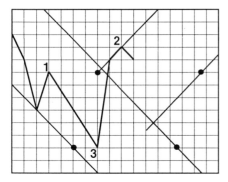

Figure 17

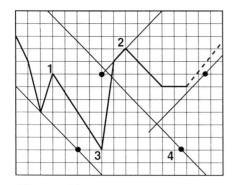

Figure 18

Target Day Within the Channels

Let's see how *target day* relates to the channels.

In Figure 15, the transition has taken place from the down-channel to the up-channel. What should you do now? First, mark the last high in the down-channel as point **1**.

Note: Point **1** need only be a sideways interruption (see dotted line) to qualify as point **1**.

Second, mark the first high in the up-channel as point **2** (see Figure 16).

Prices have now entered the pivotal area. (See Figure 12 for location of the pivotal areas.)

Third, point **3** is the last low in the down-channel following point **1** (see Figure 17).

Points **1** and **3** will always be in the same channel; point **2** will always be in the opposite channel.

Finally, count the number of days between points **1** and **2**. Then add the same number of days to point **3** to arrive at point **4**—*target day.* Or, using the more convenient **PAMA Method**, count the days between points **1** and **3** and add that number to point **2**. This will also give you point **4**—*target day.* Thus, 1, 3 = 2, 4. This concept of counting for *target day* is so important that the previous charts (Figures 15 through 18) have been reversed (Figures 19 through 22) to help you fully understand the procedure.

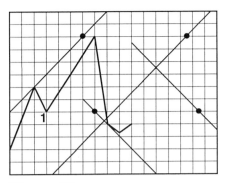

Figure 19

First, mark the last low in the up-channel point **1** (see Figure 19).

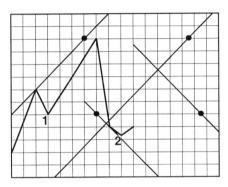

Figure 20

Second, mark the first low in the down-channel point **2** (see Figure 20).

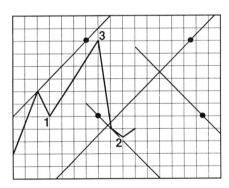

Figure 21

Third, mark the highest point in the up-channel following point **1** as point **3**. Points **1** and **3** will always be in the same channel while point **2** will always be in the opposite channel (see Figure 21).

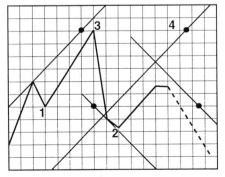

Figure 22

Finally, count the number of days between points **1** and **2**. Then add the same number of days to point **3** to arrive at point **4**—*target day*. Or, the preferred method is to count the days between points **1** and **3** and add that number to point **2** to find point **4**—*target day*.

Thus, **1, 3 = 2, 4**

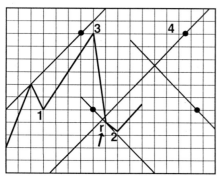

Figure 23

The Reversal Pattern

If you bought in the up-channel (see Figure 23), you would want to know when the market leaves the up-channel, which may or may not lead to a sell signal. For that reason, a small **r** (which stands for *reversal*) is placed at the exit as seen in Figure 23. This small **r** is a warning signal that a change in direction may be coming.

If, at *target day* (4), prices remain in the same channel as point **2**, then this becomes a potential reversal signal (i.e., a sell signal at day **4**). However, other factors must be considered before a sell signal can be official.

RULE: *A market can be traded only in an* **r** *channel.*

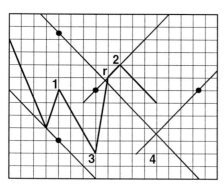

Figure 24

For a buy signal, the opposite of Figure 23 is also true, as illustrated in Figure 24.

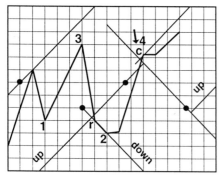

Figure 25

The Continuation Pattern

If prices emerge from the down-channel by *target day* (4), then this becomes a *continuation pattern* (i.e., prices have dodged the down-channel and have resumed their upward momentum). Place a small **c** (which stands for *continuation*) where the market exits from the down-channel (see Figure 25).

RULE: *Once in a c channel, the market cannot be traded.*

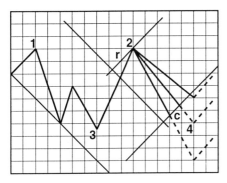

The opposite of the situation illustrated in Figure 25 is also true. **Continuation** patterns can exit anywhere outside the channel by *target day* (**4**) as indicated by the dotted lines in Figure 26.

Figure 26

Deviations

So far, you have seen only charts that follow the perfect **1, 2 = 3, 4** formula. Unfortunately, the formula is not always exact. For example, if the number of days between points **1** and **3** are less than three days, then that number of days would be considered abnormally few. Chances are, as a reaction, the number of days between points **2** and **4** would be considerably greater. To compensate for these abnormalities, certain adjustments called *deviations* need to be made.

Deviations are the real secrets of this system. They are the means of bringing market cycles into closer alignment with the **1, 2 = 3, 4** formula.

RULE: *Unless otherwise stated, there can be no less than three days between points 1 and 3.*

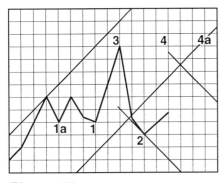

Figure 27 illustrates the above rule. Point **1** is the *last low* in the up-channel. Point **3** is the *highest high* in the up-channel. The rule calls for more than two days between **1** and **3**; so you must extend point **1** to **1a** This allows five days between **1a** and **3**. Extend point **2** five days to the right to find *target day* at **4a**.

1a, 3 = 2, 4a

Figure 27

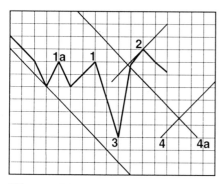

Figure 28

By reversing channel directions, you still have only two days between points **1** and **3**; so you must extend point **1** to **1a**. This allows five days between **1a** and **3**. Extend point **2** five days to the right to find ***target day*** at **4a**.

1a, 3 = 2, 4a

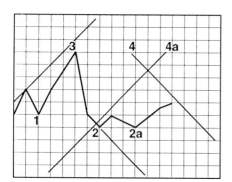

Figure 29

As you will discover later, it will be necessary to extend other areas besides points **1** and **3**. One such area is **2** and **2a**. Point **2** is the *first low in the down-channel*, and **2a** is the next low in the down-channel. ***Target day*** (**4a**) is found by the formula:

1, 3 = 2a, 4a

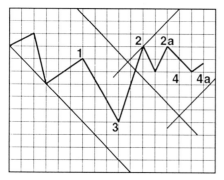

Figure 30

Again, Figure 30 shows a reverse channel direction from the previous figure. The same rules apply: Point **2** is the ***first high in the up-channel.*** Point **2a** is next to the first high in the up-channel. Point **4a** is found by adding the same number of days between points **1** and **3** as there is between points **2a** and **4a**.

Thus, **1, 3 = 2a, 4a**

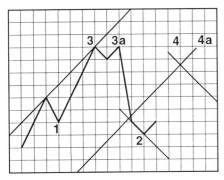

Figure 31

Point **3** is the ***highest high in the up-channel following point 1***. Point **3a** must be at the same price level as point **3**, or very close to it. If this occurs, then either high may be used for measuring. To find point **4a**, simply add the days between points **1** and **3a** to point **2** (see Figure 31).

Thus, **1, 3a = 2, 4a**

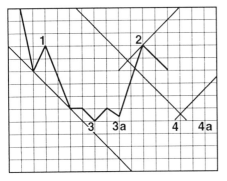

Figure 32

Point **3** or point **3a** is the ***lowest low in the down-channel following point 1***. Either point may be used for measuring. If you use **1, 3** for measuring, add four days to **2** to find **4**. If you use **1, 3a** for measuring, add six days to point **2** to find point **4a**, which is ***target day*** (see Figure 32).

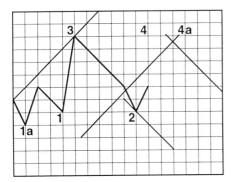

Figure 33

Why all the concern over the positions of points **1** and **3**? Figure 33 illustrates what can happen when there is only one day between points **1** and **3**. Add one day to point **2** and guess what happens? ***Target day*** has already arrived! It is now impossible to clear the down-channel at ***target day*** (**4**).

By extending point **1** to **1a**, you automatically increase the number of days between points **1** and **3** by at least three days. In this case, there are now four days to ***target day*** and plenty of time to form a ***continuation pattern***.

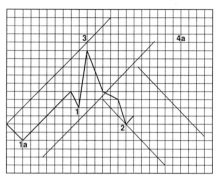

Figure 34 demonstrates how far back you might have to go before finding a **1a** low. Also notice how far away **4a** had to be placed.

Figure 34

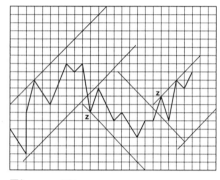

After leaving an up-channel or down-channel, the **z** (which stands for ***corner zigzag***) reverses direction for a day (see Figure 35). From there it quickly resumes its original direction past the point marked **z**. It tends to cling close to the channel lines as if in a corner. ***The zigzag formation cannot be used in measuring.*** (Exceptions to the rule will be explained later. See Figures 44 and 63.)

Figure 35

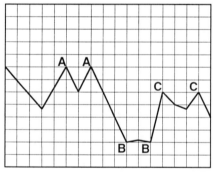

In Figure 36, notice the double top at **A** and the double bottom at **B**. Each top/bottom gives you an option from which point to measure. Usually only two days are involved; however, sometimes three days are involved, such as seen at **C**. The formation between **AA** and **CC** need not be double tops/bottoms, but can be flat as seen at **BB**.

Figure 36

Review of Deviation

Deviations are designed to adjust to the various phases of a market cycle for the purpose of aligning it as closely as possible to the ideal **1, 3 = 2, 4** formula.

Instead of drawing trendlines, moving averages, relative strengths, stochastics, etc., the ***PAMA Method*** is revolutionary because its only concern is whether or not the **2, 4** side of the equation is stronger than the **1, 3** side: If stronger, it usually leads to a buying opportunity, and vice versa.

The principles of ***deviation*** allow for flexibility in the system, which becomes vitally important as it relates to the second factor—***support and resistance***.

Support and Resistance

The choice of which ***target day*** to use is greatly influenced by ***support and resistance***.

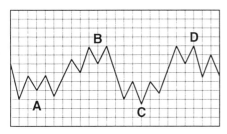

Figure 37

Quite simply, **A** and **C** are ***support*** areas while **B** and **D** are ***resistance*** areas, as illustrated in Figure 37. There is no rule on just how far back in time these major areas of support and resistance cease to influence current prices. However, experience shows that the most recent four months supply sufficient data for our purposes.

In Figure 37, look at the **A** area where traders bought and sold in large numbers. Those who bought at **A** rejoiced to see their purchase rise to **B**, where once again, the bulls and bears battled it out. At this point, prices entered the ***pivotal area*** where it is critical to determine if the market is going to continue higher or drop in price. In this case, prices dropped from **B** to **C**. Point **A** obviously offered support for the **C** area and presented a buying opportunity. When prices went from **C** to **D**, they met with resistance from **B**.

Of course, it is not mandatory to buy or sell just because of nearby support or resistance. A ***continuation pattern*** will overcome these areas at some point in time. It is not unusual to see prices go right through heavy support or resistance areas without leaving their channel.

Another support/resistance situation comes when prices reach round numbers (e.g., 1000, 2500, 3000). For example, if the **B** area were 3000, and you made a purchase in the **C** area, you could expect strong resistance in the **D** area.

Support and Resistance in Action

NEW HIGH: Price has reached a new high within the past four months, or there is no significant resistance for the past four months.

NEW LOW: Price has dropped to a new low within the past four months, or there is no significant support for the past four months.

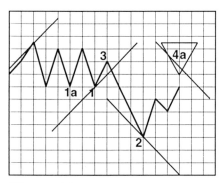

Figure 38

From points **1** to **3**, there is only one day, and since three days are a minimum requirement, an extension to **1a** is necessary (see Figure 38). The price at *target day* (**4a**) is now close to the down-channel's upper line, but is still in the down-channel. With all that overhead resistance, it would be risky to hold. *Sell.*

1a, 3 = 2, 4a

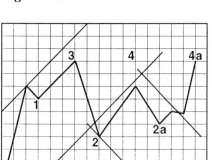

Figure 39

Let's say that point **3** is at a four-month high (see Figure 39). When *target day* (**4**) arrived, the price was still in the down-channel. However, with so little resistance, do not sell—wait for the next low at **2a**. This allows **4** to be extended to **4a**. Prices then clear the down-channel. *Never sell in an up-channel.*

1, 3 = 2a, 4a

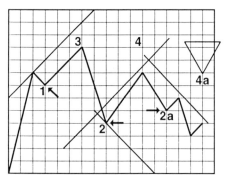

Figure 40

Figure 40 is the same as Figure 39 except for the outcome at **4a**. The down-channel was still not penetrated at *target day* (**4a**). The *local support* was gone as shown by the arrows. Sell at *target day* (**4a**).

LOCAL SUPPORT: At least three points of support have been broken in the past month. Or just two points have been broken if both of these are strong areas of support.

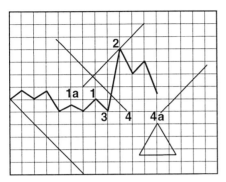

Figure 41

Figure 41 shows a buy signal. The last high in the down-channel would allow only one day between point **1** and **3**. Since there are not at least three days, go back to the next highest and label it point **1a**. On *target day* (**4a**), the price nestled nicely into the support area. ***Buy.***

1a, 3 = 2, 4a

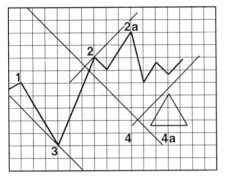

Figure 42

Target day has another aspect that must be considered. Supposing prices are going up at *target day* (**4**). Do not buy on such a rise. Wait for prices to drop toward **4a**. (See Figure 42.)

Important Sell Signal

In Figure 43, the reverse of Figure 42, it is too risky to wait for **4a**. *Sell at target day* (**4**) if local support has been broken and there is no important support during the past four months. Do not sell just because points of support have been penetrated. Wait for *target day* (**4**).

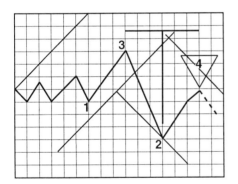

Figure 43

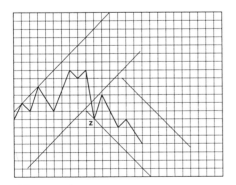

Figure 44

Figure 44 shows an exception—where local support has been broken by a *zigzag*, the rules governing *zigzags* can be ignored.

Summary and the New Look

Let's conclude this discussion on support and resistance by summarizing all that has been learned so far. First, you were introduced to the idea of the equation **1, 2 = 3, 4**, which taught you the mechanics of finding *target day*. Since this equation is by no means perfect, *deviations* were introduced to compensate for some inaccuracies. This involved much labeling and possible confusion, but this will be simplified.

From there, you evaluated market action with the **1, 3 = 2, 4** formula instead of **1, 2 = 3, 4**. The reason was illustrated in Figure 33, where the first consideration was to make certain of the proper relationship between points **1** and **3**. The second consideration was the relationship between points **2** and **4**. It is natural and convenient, therefore, to lump points **1** and **3** together and points **2** and **4** together so that **1, 3 = 2, 4**.

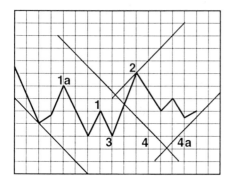

Figure 45

Figure 45 shows the way charts looked previously.

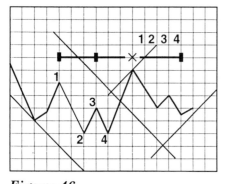

Figure 46

Figure 46 illustrates the new look and the steps to follow:

1. Mark the first top after a channel break with an **X** alert.

2. Draw a line left of **X** to the last high in the down-channel (**3**). It is less than three days to the lowest low (**4**), therefore

3. Extend the line to the next high in the down channel (**1**). It is now at least three days to the lowest low (**4**).

4. In this case, add four days (marked **1, 2, 3, 4**) to the right of **X** to find *target day*.

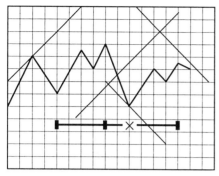

Figure 47

By reversing channel directions, the **X** and its extension will appear at the bottom (see Figure 47).

Note: From now on, the two marks left of **X** and its extensions will show the days between the *high* and *low* points which, in turn, will equal the days to the right of **X**. These notations are quick, easy and efficient!

Buy and Sell Signals

Target day and the *support/resistance* areas are closely linked together. Next, we will examine this relationship and formulate definite buy and sell signals. Finally, the third principle—called the *"T"*—will be added for an independent confirmation of the *target* signal.

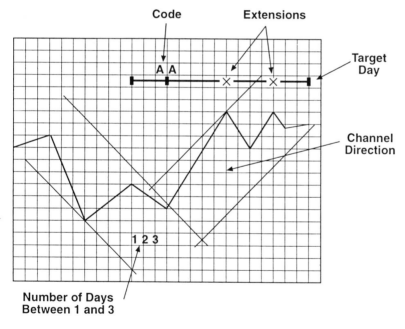

Figure 48

The format for explaining the various signals (illustrated in Figure 48) follows: Above the line to the left of the **X** is a code describing your plan of action. This forces you to think through the situation at hand before making any decision.

Although this process may appear a bit complicated, it's really quite simple and logical. With a little patience, the pieces will fall neatly into place.

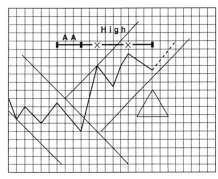

Figure 49

Codes for Buy Signals

AA   Up-channel—buy

New high within past four months

Three days minimum

XX

Figure 49 illustrates the following situation: A new high has just been formed, and you want to purchase this market. Since it is very high, you will want to give it every opportunity to back off and enter a down-channel. With that in mind, wait for a second top (**X**) and its *target day* before you buy. This could trigger a rather strong buy signal.

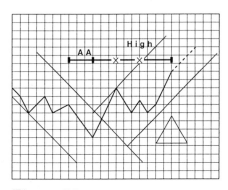

Figure 50

The situation in Figure 50 is the same as Figure 49 except that the price has moved up through local resistance at *target day*. Both Figures 50 and 49 show valid **AA** buy signals.

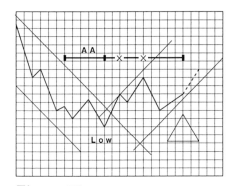

Figure 51

AA   Up-channel—buy

Up from a low with no important support for four months

Three days minimum

XX

This is where the system begins to shine! Consider Figure 51. Prices dropped to where there was no important support for four months. As soon as the price enters the up-channel, label the first top with an **X**. Then see if there are the minimum three days between points **1** and **3**. In this situation, there were only two days, so look for the next little top. Now there are five days between points

1a and **3**. Wait for one more top in the up-channel to provide the next **X** extension. Finally, you are in a position to find *target day*.

Notice how automatic this decision becomes: First, you received advance notice that a good opportunity might be near when the up-channel was reached. Next, you knew to the day when to take action provided the up-channel was not violated. Of course, the price might drop out of the up-channel the next day, but a nice base for support has already been built. Most technicians would wait for the overhead resistance to be eliminated before buying. The *PAMA Method*, however, will often get you aboard while still in the *pivotal area*, thus capturing many more points.

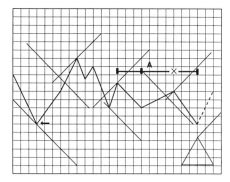

Figure 52

A   Up-channel—buy

One other *significant* low at about the same price level

Three days minimum

X

In Figure 52, the arrow points to one other important low, or low area. Preferably, the low should occur before the last down-channel, but this is not mandatory. This creates a moderate amount of support, and only one **X** is needed.

Within an **A** code, prices are not necessarily coming up from a four-month low.

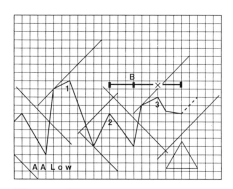

Figure 53

B   Up-channel—buy

1. Up-channel from **AA** low

2. Down-channel—not lower than the **AA** low

3. Up-channel forming **B**

Three days minimum

X

The sequence starts from an **AA** low, and is followed by a second low not as low as **AA**. The three steps outlined in Figure 53 generally occur in rapid succession. The outlook for **B** is most favorable because it places the purchase well within the pivotal area. Besides, the up-and-down movement creates excellent support.

Unlike **A**, **B** is coming up from a four-month low.

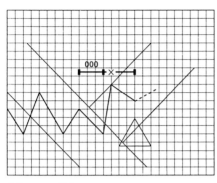

Figure 54

000   Up-channel—buy

Triple bottom

Two days minimum

X

In Figure 54, this signal is characterized by three distinct bottoms, all close to the same price level. These bottoms may be spread throughout the past four months, or they can be bunched together within the local support area of one month. If the bottoms were bunched together more than one month ago, then they have lost much of their power of support and should be treated as an **A** support signal. Ignore the ***zigzag*** rule. The ***triple bottom*** is more important.

> **RULE:** *To qualify as a **triple bottom**, there must be at least five days between each bottom.*

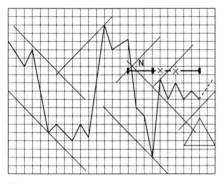

Figure 55

N   Up-channel—buy

Neutral—a buy signal that comes between equally strong support and resistance

Three days minimum

XX

It would seem that if a market were poised equally between support and resistance, there would be about a 50/50 chance as to the future direction of the market. Experience has taught, however, that the direction can be quite accurately determined using the principles of the system (see Figure 55).

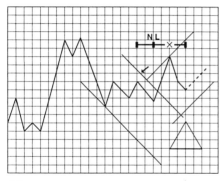

Figure 56

NL   Up-channel—buy

The last high in the down-channel has been penetrated on the first **X**.

Two days minimum

X

Figure 56 is the same as Figure 55 except that the first **X** closes above the last high in the down-channel. Since this is a stronger pattern than shown in Figure 55, only one **X** and two days are required. If there is strong resistance nearby, revert back to the weaker *neutral* signal.

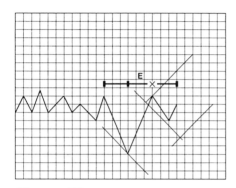

Figure 57

E   Up-channel

Do not buy because of overhead resistance (see Figure 57).

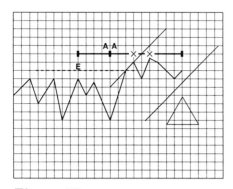

Figure 58

If prices penetrate the **E** level (see Figure 58), then treat it as an **AA** code (see Figure 49). The **E** area now offers strong support.

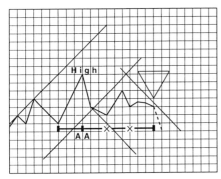

Figure 59

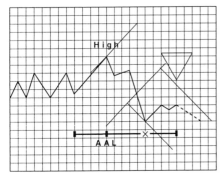

Figure 60

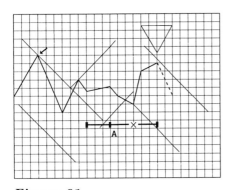

Figure 61

Codes for Sell Signals

AA   Down-channel—sell

New high (or no resistance) for past four months

Three days minimum

XX

In Figure 59, a new high was reached within the past four months. Obviously, this market is still in a strong upward mode. To give it every opportunity to resume its upward momentum, it is necessary to give it **XX** and three days before selling.

AAL   Down-channel—sell

Local support broken with first **X**

Three days minimum

X

In Figure 60, after coming off a *new high* within the past four months, prices drop *swiftly* through local support (see Figure 40). If prices, however, take many days and just meander through local support, the **AAL** signal could be a simple **AA**. This is a matter of using your own judgment.

A   Down-channel—sell

One other *significant* high at about the same price level

Three days minimum

X

In Figure 61, the arrow points to one other important high, or high area. Preferably, the high should occur before the last up-channel, but it is not mandatory. This creates a moderate amount of resistance, and so only one **X** is needed. With an **A** code, prices are not necessarily coming down from a four-month high.

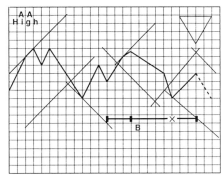

Figure 62

B   Down-channel-sell

1. Down-channel from **AA** high

2. Up-channel—not higher than **AA** high

3. Down-channel forming **B**

Three days minimum

X

In Figure 62, the sequence starts from an **AA** high and is followed by a second high not as high as **AA**. The three steps outlined in Figure 62 generally occur in rapid succession.

The position of **B** is excellent because it places the sale well within the pivotal area. Besides, the up-and-down movement creates strong overhead resistance. Unlike **A**, **B** is coming down from a four-month high.

RULE: *To qualify as a **triple top**, there must be at least five days between each top.*

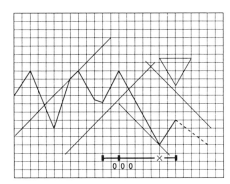

Figure 63

000   Down-channel—sell

Triple top

Two days minimum

X

In Figure 63, this signal is characterized by three or more distinct tops, all close to the same price level. These tops may be spread throughout the past four months, or they may be bunched together within the local resistance area of one month. If they were bunched together more than one month ago, then they will have lost much of their power of resistance and should be treated as an **A**. Ignore the ***zigzag*** rule. The ***triple top*** is more important.

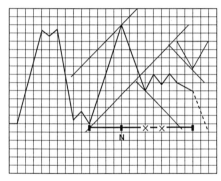

Figure 64

N   Down-channel—sell

Neutral—a sell signal that comes between equally strong support and resistance

Three days minimum

XX

In Figure 64, it would seem that if a market were poised equally between **support and resistance** there would be a 50/50 chance as to the future direction of the market. However, experience has taught that the direction can be quite accurately determined using the principles of the **PAMA Method**.

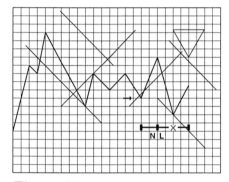

Figure 65

NL   Down-channel—sell

The *last low* in the up-channel has been penetrated on the *first* **X**.

Two days minimum.

X

The situation in Figure 65 is the same as in Figure 64 except that the first **X** closes below the last low in the up-channel. Since this is a weaker position than a plain **neutral**, only one **X** and two days are required. If there is strong support in the area, revert back to a **neutral** signal.

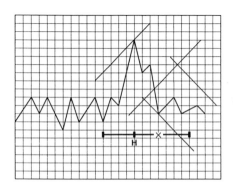

Figure 66

H   Down-channel—do not sell

Hold—a sell signal that comes close to a strong support area.

When a market approaches a strong support area, it is best to see if that area will hold after a sell signal (see Figure 66).

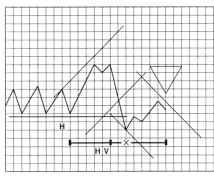

Figure 67

HV   Down-channel—sell

HV (*hold violated*)

Three days minimum

X

Figure 67 is a follow-up on the preceding chart (Figure 66). If the area does not hold, sell with one **X** and at least three days. Obviously, some serious resistance has now come into play. Depending on your temperament, you may want to sell at the breaking of the **hold** signal.

The "T" and Its Construction

The third factor in the *PAMA Method's* pivotal area is called the *"T"*. As with the *target*, the *"T"* has a basic symmetry found on most charts. As prices fluctuate up and down, they tend to be somewhat symmetrical in size, shape and relative position. These two factors—the *target* and the *"T"*—measure the same thing, only from slightly different approaches.

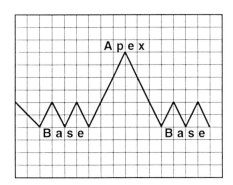

Figure 68

Figure 68 shows an ideal triangular shape with the apex at the top and the bases on either side forming the corners of the triangle.

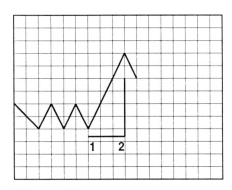

Figure 69

First, draw a vertical line down from the apex of the triangle past the base. Connect points **1** and **2** (see Figure 69).

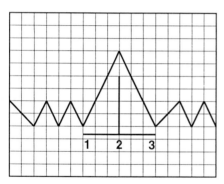

Figure 70

Next, extend line **1, 2** to **3** so that **1, 2 = 2, 3**. Now you have an inverted **"T"**. Point **3** indicates a day that prices will possibly reverse (see Figure 70).

Deviations of the "T"

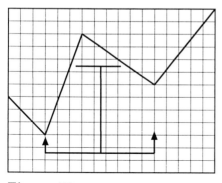

Figure 71

Figure 71 shows a rather flat base on the left side. Measure just the bottom of the triangle and do not include the base. An exception: If the left side of the base has a day or two of no price change, then you have an option of extending the base.

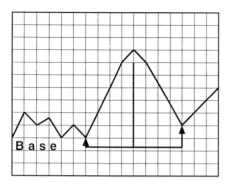

Figure 72

Often you will find the triangles are not symmetrical, as shown in Figure 72. When this becomes evident, draw a horizontal line and drop a vertical line as before. This is called a **mid-"T"** signal.

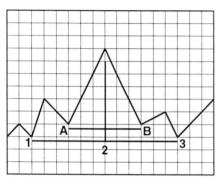

Figure 73

In the instance shown in Figure 73, you have the option of using the **A, B** measurement or the **1, 2, 3. A** is actually a part of the left wall; thus, the **1, 2, 3** is the preferred measurement. In practice, the choice between **A, B** and **1, 2, 3** is made when *target day* has been established. The closest measurement to *target day* is the one that would be used.

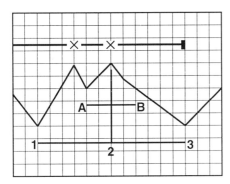

Figure 74

When coordinating with an **AA** *target day*, a *"T"* is used only at the second **X** (see Figure 74). Here again, an **A, B** or a **1, 2, 3** choice needs to be made. Obviously, in this case, use the **1, 2, 3** *"T"*, which coincides with *target day*.

The *"T"* is an integral part of the analysis within the *pivotal area*. Since it is not as flexible as the *target*, it becomes a stabilizing influence for the entire pivotal area. Also, it acts as a confirmation for the *target*, and indeed, it influences the decision to either widen or narrow the *target day*. If the *target day* and the *"T" day* agree, then the chances of a price reversal is greater than if there were many days in between. In any event, it is best to check the *"T"* before making a buy or sell decision.

The "T" Signals

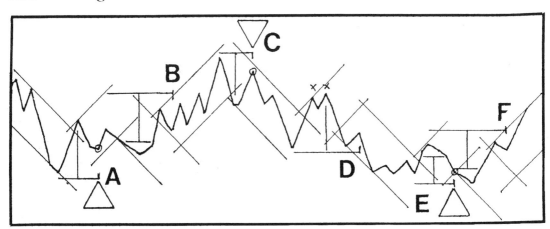

Figure 75

Figure 75 displays just the *"T"* signals in a variety of ways that are commonly found in charting.

A—The first signal is a simple three days up and three days down for a buy signal.

B—The channel break was quickly corrected by the *"T"* whose arm extended into the up-channel.

C—The channel break at **C** brought a sell signal because the *"T"* remained well within the down-channel.

D—If *target day* calls for a double **X**, always use the second **X** for constructing the *"T"*.

E—Since the downside of the breakout was shallower than the upside, a *mid-"T"* was constructed for a buy signal. The price slipped into the down-channel, which challenged the buy signal.

F—A *"T"* cleared the down-channel.

The "T", Target Day and Support/Resistance

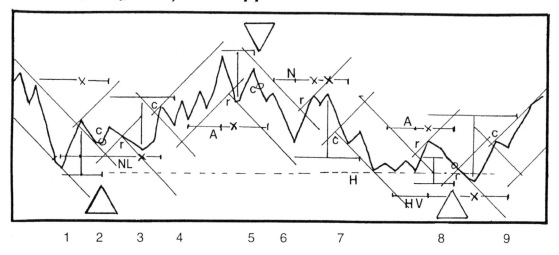

Figure 76

Figure 76 shows the same chart as the one demonstrating the *"T"* (see Figure 75) only this time all three signals have been blended together to form an outstanding trading program. The numbers below the chart refer to the explanation of the signals.

1—When starting a chart without any history, use any undesignated label until sufficient data are available for a proper code.

2—*Target day* came one day later than the *"T"*. Either day could be used for a buy signal. A small **c** is placed above the signal to show that no further trade can be made as long as the price remains in the up-channel.

3—The price then dropped into the down-channel. Place a small **r** at the channel exit to show that it could lead to a sell signal.

4—Without sufficient data a number of codes could have been used. It was decided to use a *neutral* with an **L** because the price had dropped through the last low in the down-channel at the first **X**. Both *target day* and the *"T"* cleared the down-channel.

5—All was well until the up-channel was violated. Place the **r** in position and then construct a *"T"*.

6—***Target day*** for an **A** label needs three days and one **X**. The last low provided only two days, and so the next to the last low brought it to five days. Since ***target day*** and the *"T"* were two days apart, split the difference and sell on the day between the two signals. Again, note the position of the **c**.

7—The next up-channel is labeled **N** for ***neutral*** because prices were tucked between ***support and resistance*** of about equal strength. Since ***neutral*** calls for **XX** and three-days, the second **X** took the price out of the up-channel, which resulted in a ***continuation pattern*** to the downside.

8—Since the downside of the breakout was shallower than the upside, a ***mid-"T"*** was constructed for a buy signal. ***Target day*** agreed with the *"T"*. Be sure you understand the measurements of target day. An **A** code was used because of one other low area at **(1)**.

9—After the buy signal, a ***hold*** was placed under the support level dating back to area **(1)**. Prices then dropped through ***hold*** creating a **HV** signal. ***Target day*** and the *"T"* confirmed a ***continuation pattern***.

Tips and Procedures

Let's take a look at how the system can be used on a day-to-day basis.

When you are ready to track your own charts, try to be as neat and as accurate as possible. Draw the channels with a well-sharpened pencil or an automatic pencil with a .05 #B lead. Mark the price changes in ink so as not to erase them by mistake. For added neatness, which promotes accuracy, use a straight edge to draw the *"T"* and ***target day*** lines.

If you are following a stock or mutual fund that reasonably mirrors the Dow, an aggressive trade would be as follows: Supposing the Dow is in an up-channel with a *"c"* designation, but at the same time, your issue is lagging in a down-channel. Buy the first day the issue enters the up-channel. This move will often allow you to enter closer to the bottom of the cycle. The opposite is true for a chance to exit nearer the top.

I follow the Dow, S&P 500 and the Benham Target 2005. I use the Dow to keep track of what is happening during the day on radio and TV. I use the S&P 500, which is a much broader index, to gauge the general market. If the Dow and S&P 500 conflict, I lean in favor of the S&P 500. The third index that I keep is the Benham Target 2005. As a member of the Benham family of mutual funds, it is most useful in tracking interest rates. There are certainly many more indices that could be followed, but I prefer to keep things as simple as possible.

I have been asked if I ever deviate from the rules when the media broadcasts news that will surely hurt the market. Yes, occasionally, I act on a news bulletin, and generally, I regret having done so. For example, only recently, the government announced that it would close down over the budget debate. I quickly sold, fearing a severe sell-off, but instead, the market went up! The next day I went back in. Later, the government closed for the second time, and now being so much smarter, I stayed pat. You guessed it, the Dow then plunged 100 points!

The lesson learned is that there are so many conflicting crosscurrents influencing the markets that you will wind up hurting yourself trying to outguess them. The best advice is: Follow the system.

All **X** measurements must have a battle plan: Label each measurement with notations such as **A**, **AA**, **N** or whatever plan is appropriate. Then, as a channel is violated, determine if you are entering the new channel with a **c** or an **r**. *Keep up to date on all measurements.*

At times you might be confused as to your next move. If so, take a few minutes to review the checklist (see page 149) or the basic instructions. From there, you might look over the Dow charts for similar situations. The market, however, is much like a hand of bridge: You never quite get the same cards twice!

What about a highly volatile issue that hardly ever stays in its channel long enough to get a good read on it? After a page of such volatility, rescale it so it does conform to the channel. In contrast, if an issue just lumbers along having difficulty showing any spikes or dips that you can label, then again, you may have to rescale it for greater volatility. There may be several months in which your issue is not displaying its usual volatility—either too much or too little. This is not a serious problem as a rule because the system is quite capable of maneuvering around these situations. However, you may decide to rescale it, and the easiest way to do this is to double or divide the number of squares from what it had been.

What should you do if your issue drops because of an ex-dividend? Unless you suspect there was a big price move, just raise the price scale at the day of the ex-dividend. This keeps the channel intact as if nothing happened. It also keeps the proper relationship between the present price and the past *support and resistance* areas.

The purpose of analyzing the Dow is to gain experience in all kinds of market conditions. By learning the rules with the Dow, you will be better prepared to tackle the more profitable futures market in Section III.

If, however, you wish to remain in the stock market, you might consider opening an account with Charles Schwab, or a similar discount company that allows you to trade hundreds of no-load mutual funds without charge. There are many services that recommend good no-load funds (i.e., Morningstar). Some may even be carried at your local library. Find the fund that suits your needs, and trade with a discount broker at no charge—a good combination.

It should be pointed out that Schwab charges a fee under certain circumstances, and since the company's policies change from time to time, it is best to contact them at 800-435-4000 for a prospectus. Another thought—it might be worthwhile to go with a family of funds and trade within the family. Even here you may be limited to the number of trades per year, especially the no-load funds. The prestigious American Funds, however, allow as many trades by telephone as you wish. The company charges a stiff entry fee, but charges nothing to switch within the fund. Furthermore, its expense ratio to net assets is very low. Call 800-325-3590.

If you are impressed with the way the **PAMA Method** can beat the Dow Jones Industrials, how would you like to trade it? Well, you can. The ASM Fund invests almost exclusively in the Dow 30 stocks. It is a no-load fund, and you can make as many as six trades a year with no charge to enter or exit. The fund does have operating expenses that will cause its return to be somewhat lower than the overall return of the index, but the advantage is that radio and television can keep you posted during the day. This allows you to make a decision without having to wait for the next day's newspaper. The fund requires that you call one-half hour before the closing bell. Call 800-445-2763 for a prospectus. Also, ask for a prospectus on the money market fund.

The Ultimate Trading Fund?

There is a way you can profit in a downmarket: Rydex is a family of funds. Rydex Nova is a no-load stock fund that should be bought when the market is going up. Rydex Ursa, on the other hand, should be bought when the market is going down. This no-load fund invests in a number of ways to take advantage of bear markets. One possible drawback: Rydex requires $10,000 to participate.

If you trade Nova and Ursa separately, you will find Nova about twice as volatile as Ursa. The easiest, and the recommended way, is to switch when the system gives a buy or sell signal for the Dow Industrials.

Call 800-820-0888 for a prospectus.

Buy Signal Summary

Channel Position	Plan	Market Position	Extensions	Target Day (Minimum)
Up	AA	New high within past four months	XX	3 days
Up	AA	New low within past four months	XX	3 days
Up	A	One other low at about the same price level	X	3 days
Up	B	Sequence:		
		1) Up-channel from AA low		
		2) Down-channel		
		3) Up-channel forming B	X	3 days
Up	000	*Triple bottom* within past four months	X	2 days
Up	N	*Neutral*—a buy signal that comes between equally strong support and resistance	XX	3 days
Up	NL	Same as *neutral* except the last high in the down-channel has been penetrated on the first X	X	2 days
Up	E	Avoid all buy signals below E because of strong resistance	–	*Do Not Buy*

Sell Signal Summary

Channel Direction	Plan	Market Position	Extensions	Target Day (Minimum)
Down	**AA**	New high within the past four months	XX	3 days
Down	**AAL**	Local support (from a high) broken with first **X**	X	3 days
Down	**H**	*Hold*—a sell signal (at a low) that comes close to strong support	–	*Do Not Sell*
Down	**HV**	*Hold violated*—The strong support at *hold* has been violated	X	3 days
Down	**A**	One other high at about the same price level.	X	3 days
Down	**B**	Sequence: 1) Down-channel from AA high 2) Up-channel 3) Down-channel	X	3 days
Down	**000**	Triple top within past four months	X	2 days
Down	**N**	*Neutral*—sell signal that comes between equally strong support and resistance	XX	3 days
Down	**NL**	Same as *neutral* except the last low in the up-channel has been penetrated on the first X	X	2 days

Section II

The Dow Jones Industrial Average 1987–1996

••••

Buy/Sell Summary

Update

Buy/Sell Summary

The table that follows provides a summary of the buy/sell signals for the Dow Jones Industrials from January 1987 to March 1995. The study began with $10,000 and ended with $40,685.

Buy Date	Buy	Sale Date	Sold	Profit
Jan. 1987	1900	Sept. 1987	2610	$13,736
Dec. 1987	1870	July 1988	2090	15,353
Aug. 1988	2000	Oct. 1989	2660	20,421
Nov. 1989	2670	Dec. 1989	2730	20,882
Feb. 1990	2630	July 1990	2870	22,788
Nov. 1990	2450	Dec. 1990	2620	24,369
Jan. 1991	2660	Nov. 1991	3075	28,170
Jan. 1992	3160	June 1992	3310	29,509
Oct. 1992	3230	Feb. 1994	3900	35,630
May 1994	3695	Sept. 1994	3845	37,076
Dec. 1994	3720	March 1995	4082	40,685

**Dow Jones Industrials
Buy and Hold**

Buy Date	Buy	Sale Date	Sold	Profit
Jan. 1987	1900	March 1995	4082	$21,484

1. Just to get started, an undesignated buy signal was used.

2. Assuming that this was a new high within the past four months, an **AA** signal came with the breaking of the up-channel in February. Prices, however, quickly resumed their upward momentum. The next break was uncertain, so an **X** was placed in position. Under the **AA** plan, a second **X** cleared the down-channel.

3. More **AA** signals were repeated until April, at which time a channel break took out the local support. This called for an **AAL** label. Notice the tiny zigzag near the exit.

4. Once again, prices rebounded using a **B** designation.

5. It was not long before prices dropped to 2210 looking more and more like a bear market. Support was gone, not only locally, but for the past two months. An **H** (*hold*) at 2235 gave way to an **HV** signal. The Dow then catapulted out of the down-channel, and shortly afterwards, reached an all-time high.

   The system has done an excellent job of avoiding a premature sale that must have whipsawed many traders.

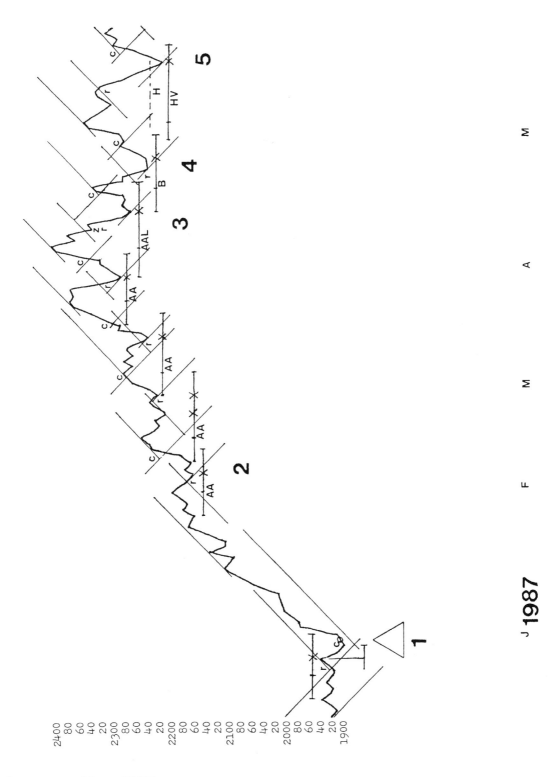

January–May 1987

6. Minor breaks in the up-channel were corrected three times with the **AA** code.

7. Something most unusual occurred following the break of the up-channel; namely, a ***corner zigzag*** cleared local support. Review Figure 35 as well as the exception to the ***zigzag*** rule (see page 19). A sale must be made as soon as possible. Sell at the *"T"* signal with the **AAL** code.

   Let's study the insert at point 7. If the zigzag had not been used for a measurement, could you still exit in time? Yes, at 2560 with an **AAL** code. After that, the breaking of the up-channel the first of October presented an **NL** code (not shown), which would allow you to escape at 2480. The ***PAMA Method*** gave you three exit possibilities!

8. The first upswing from the down-channel was labeled **AA** because it had risen from a low with no support within the past four months. Only one **X** was needed to clear the up-channel.

9. Follow this carefully: By mid-September, the Dow went into an up-channel. The first little top was a classic ***zigzag*** and could not be used for measuring. The next top was labeled a ***neutral*** rather than an NL because the last high in the down-channel was too insignificant. The second **X** with its five-day extension brought a welcome ***continuation*** pattern. The famous crash of '87 had begun!

10. As was expected, new up-channels could not hold.

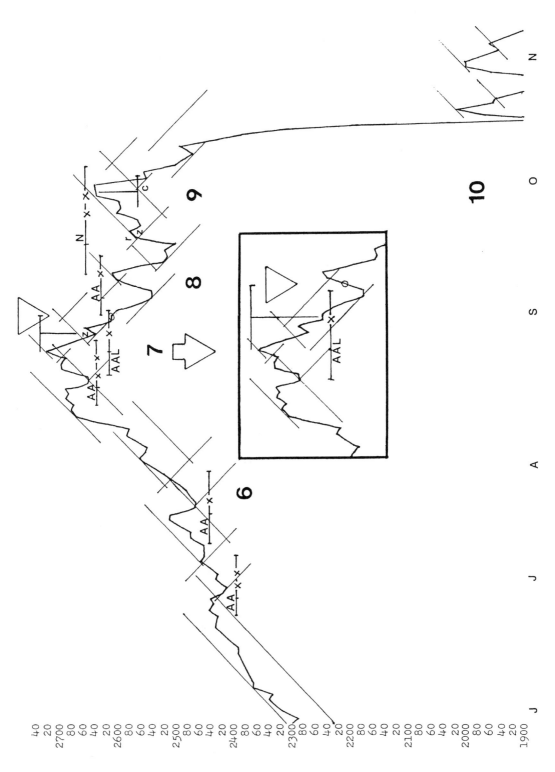

June–November 1987

11.   The graph in the insert is a carry-over from the previous graph, whch shows the low on October 19 at 1738. It was obvious that some base building would be necessary before a recovery could be expected. A double bottom formed the first part of December.

12.   A powerful up-thrust cleared the December 1 resistance, which called for an **NL** signal. This occurred exactly between the high of 2000 and the low of 1738.

13.   A triple top came because of the three tops near the 2000 level.

14.   An **AA** was used because there was no resistance for about 500 points!

15.   Two more *neutral* **L** signals avoided premature selling.

16.   The first of April was labeled **AA**. Why not **AAL** with the breaking of the local support? The reason is because of the extremely good support at 1940.

Note: The small **c** and **r** designations for *continuation* and *reversal* channels are most helpful when tracking a number of issues. As you post each issue, you will know that there is nothing more to be done if a **c** is found at the last channel break. If there is an **r**, however, it will be necessary to check your measurements for possible action. In this study, where only the Dow is being considered, the **c** and **r** notations will be dropped for the sake of simplicity except for complicated reversals.

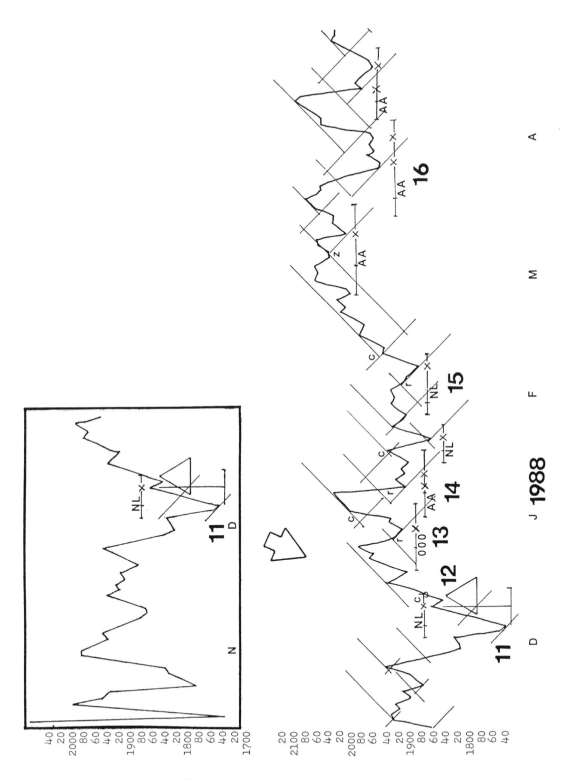

December 1987–April 1988

17. In May a **hold** signal was used because of the splendid support in the 1940–1960 area. When the price dropped below the 1940 level, an **HV** signal went into effect, thus saving an unnecessary sale.

18. An **A** acknowledged the moderate resistance at 2100 set last April.

19. The sale was a routine **AA** stemming from a new high. The sudden reversal to the upside ran into solid resistance, and so an **E** was placed in position.

20. A **neutral** **L** signal came between strong support at 1940 and equally strong resistance at 2100. An **L** was used to denote that the first **X** rose slightly above the last high in the down-channel. This allowed an excellent entry point for a purchase. The next channel break was also an **N**. The spread between support and resistance had become very narrow. Notice that there were eight days between points **1** and **3**. A second **X** was not needed.

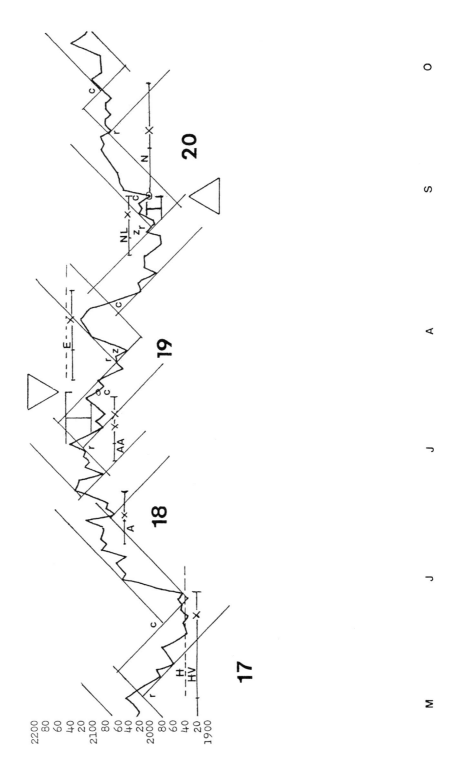

May–October 1988

21. The exit from the up-channel was not a *zigzag*. Because of the new high at 2160, an **AA** was used. A sell signal developed, but good support in August allowed a hold at 1985.

22. A tiny *zigzag* preceded the **N** signal. What about an **A** sell signal? It was a little shy of the 2160 level set back in October. When it bounced above local resistance, it seemed best to stay with the *neutral* code.

23. In February prices staged a new high followed by an **AA** signal. A **B** code sell signal was saved by a *"T"*. You might note the little double bottom on the first of March. The **B** code could have started from the second dip, which would have cleared the down-channel.

24. Here is a genuine triple top that should be sold with only two days and one **X**. Both *target day* and the *"T"* agreed on the sale date, so the symbol for the sale was placed in position. You would be justified in making the sale, but look at the support in mid-January and the first of March. This made it difficult to go ahead with the sale. The 2200 price level would also come into play. Place a hold at 2230.

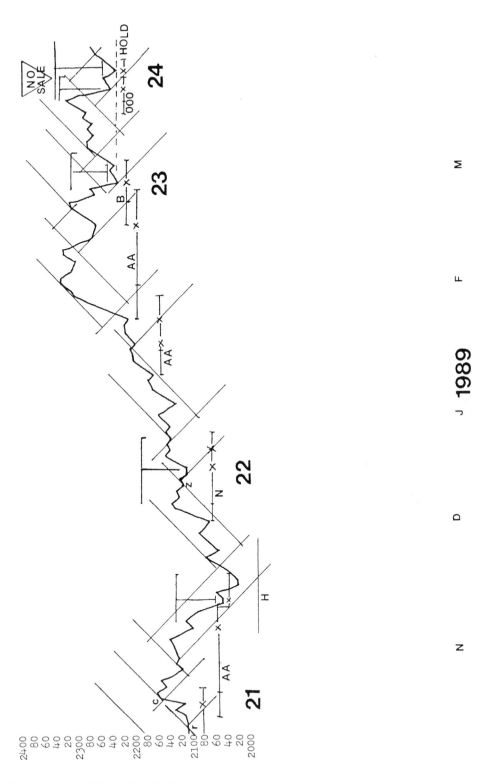

November 1988–March 1989

25. A strong rally has taken the Dow into new high territory. Mid-June suggested an **AAL** code, but prices only meandered through local support. Use an **AA** instead (see Figure 60). Pay particular attention to the price movement around July 1. Following a new high, prices dropped through local support. You would have been justified selling at the first **X** if you were counting on *target day* alone. Do not neglect to include the "*T*" in your decision making. A careful look at the area showed that the right wall was climbing much slower than the left wall had fallen. This was evident three days after the bottom of the dip. It was here that a *mid-*"*T*" should be constructed and brought into the analysis. By doing this, you would have added one more day and avoided an unnecessary sale.

   If you had sold at 2470, about the best you could have done would be to reenter at 2630 using the **AA** new high plan.

26. A new high in September was followed by a down-channel that left you two options:

   1. Use the little double bottom at 2705, for both **XX**, and then sell at *target day*.

   2. Use only one **X** for the little double bottom at 2705, and wait for the next low to use the second **X**.

   It was decided to use the second option for these reasons: The Dow, as you can see, has been in a remarkable bull market—interrupted only by periods of consolidation. Also, there was still decent support in August which, incidentally, blocked an **AAL** signal.

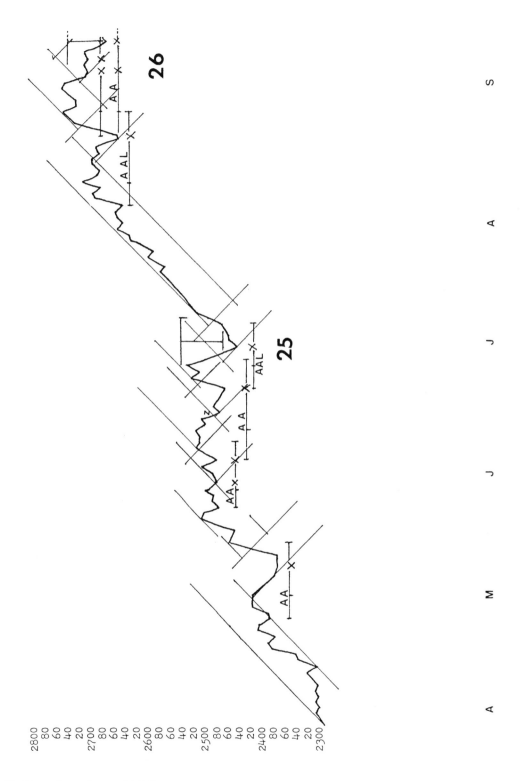

April–September 1989

27. A brand new all-time high gave way to a dramatic drop, which smashed all local resistance. The only support was 3 1/2 months ago—100 points lower. A sale was made using a **B** signal shades of October '87!

28. The market was beginning to look less ominous. A sideways move prompted an **N** signal, which resulted in breaking local resistance.

29. Looking back at the October plunge, the present price was approaching the October high. An **A** sell signal was taken.

30. The sudden spurt to a new high called for an **AA** high plan. Prices, however, could not remain in the up-channel and a severe drop ensued.

31. Even though the drop stayed within the four-month time limit, prices had fallen below most of the October–November support level. An **AA** buy, therefore, was appropriate. Since it was difficult to determine which *"T"* to use, a compromise was made between the signals. Because of the lows in the area, a ***hold*** was placed at 2540.

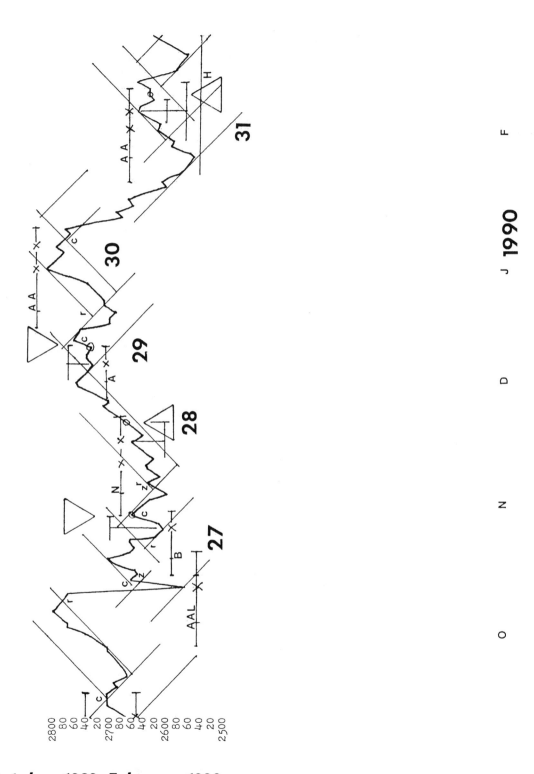

October 1989–February 1990

32. A *neutral* signal side-stepped a sale.

33. Again, a *neutral* signal cleared a nasty 100 point fall.

    This *cannot be labeled an* **AAL** because it did not originate from a four-month high.

34. The drop from the all-time high was cleared with an **AA**.

35. This is an interesting pattern. It could be a **B** code coming off a high at 34 and then back to match the high, and back down again. What you should see, however, is the decisive breaking of local support for an **AAL** sell signal.

36. With the resumption of the up-channel, an **E** was put in place only to be penetrated shortly thereafter. It took the discipline of the system not to jump in above 2920 where you would be badly whipsawed.

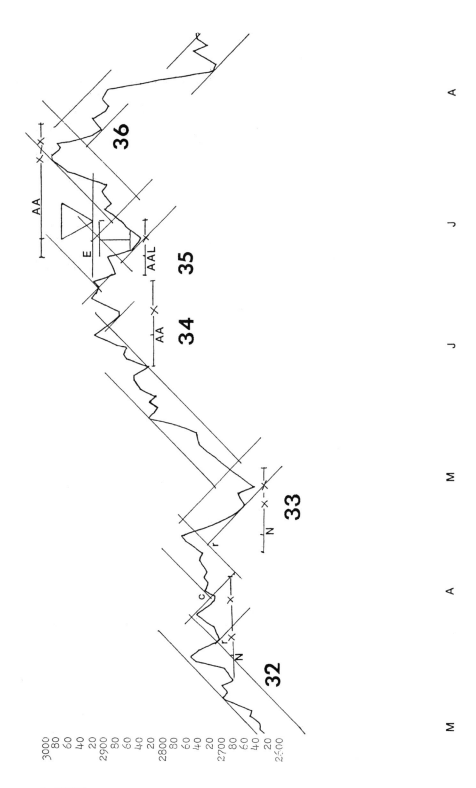

March–August 1990

37. The **AA** labels were obvious through mid-October.

38. During the first part of November, a **B** buy signal was taken well within the pivotal area. The traditional trader would have waited for prices to clear the congestion area before buying at around the 2550 level. We, on the other hand, captured an additional 100 points at 2450 with the **B** signal.

39. A *neutral* signal cleared the down-channel.

40. With the breaking of the up-channel, the price is now the same as it was last September. Since it falls within the four-month time limit, an **A** code was used. Channel construction for this signal is critical. Is the first dip really in the down-channel?

41. What a strange formation to see prices bounce back and forth 150 points just as they did last October! Were they simply testing the October lows again? The 2620 level of last September should not enter the analysis since they were no longer in the four-month time limit.

    The upsurge started from a *neutral* position and quickly shot past the last high in the down-channel for an **NL** label. The resistance of last month was worrisome, but as *target day* arrived prices firmed up, clearing the resistance somewhat.

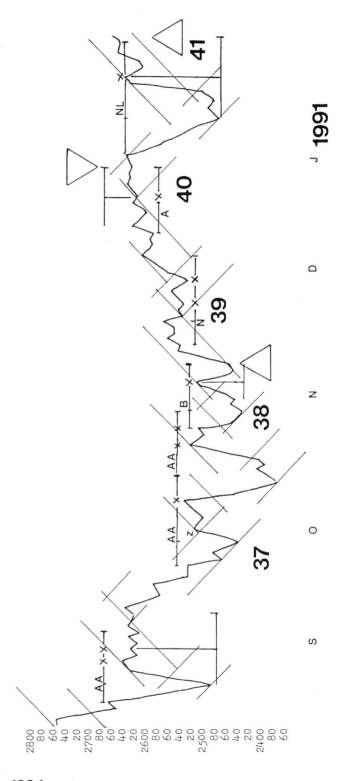

September 1990–January 1991

42. A splendid rally cleared resistance in much the same way as it did in June 1990, and at the same price level of 2900!

43. Again, the price came to within 10 points of the July 2, 1990, record-breaking high before slipping back.

44. The first **X** started out being almost an **AAL**, but penetration through 2870 was not decisive. Label it an **AA**.

45. A **B** signal cleared the down-channel.

46. An **A** signal lifted the Dow out of the down-channel, as well as an **H** later on.

47. A very questionable *zigzag* on the first of June was allowed to stay. An **AA** with a measurement of seven days took the price out of the down-channel. If you had split the *"T"* and **AA** days, you might not have cleared the down-channel, but you certainly would have placed a *hold* at 2870. Seldom do you see five lows lined up like this!

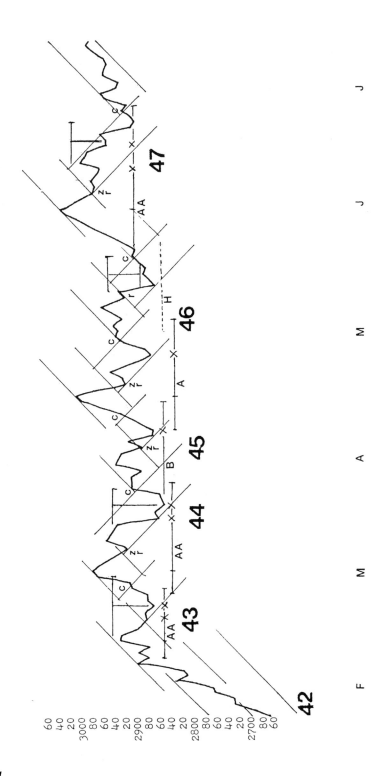

February–July 1991

48. The end of last May's high of 3040 allowed a label of **A** on the July high of 3020. In mid-August another **A** was used, only this time it was because of the low at 2900 in June.

49. In November prices rose to an established triple top (see arrows). This required two days minimum with only one **X**. The *"T"* might better have been placed at the **X** rather than making it a ***mid-"T"*** code.

50. The system is not perfect. Here, it has failed miserably! It was impossible to re-enter near the first of December.

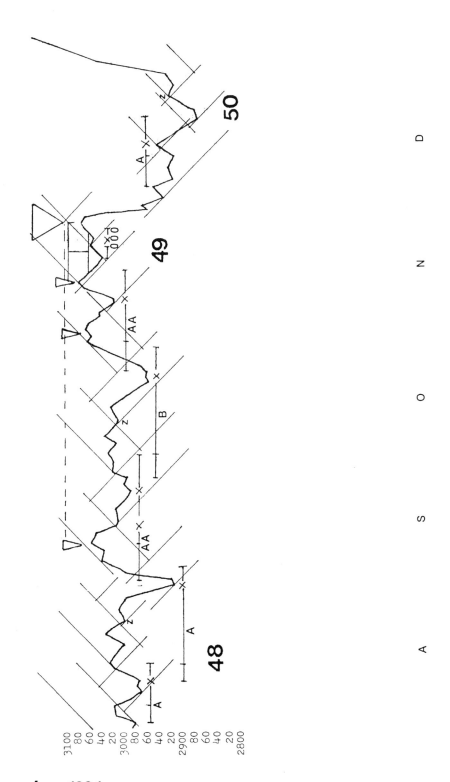

August–December 1991

51. After surging past two layers of resistance, a consolidation finally provided an entry with *"T"* and ***target day*** agreeing.

52. A series of small channel breaks created an unusually narrow trading range, which finally emerged to the upside in April.

53. In June prices took out the local support, but huge support was still available within the past four months. A sale seemed appropriate because this support may be as much as 100 points lower.

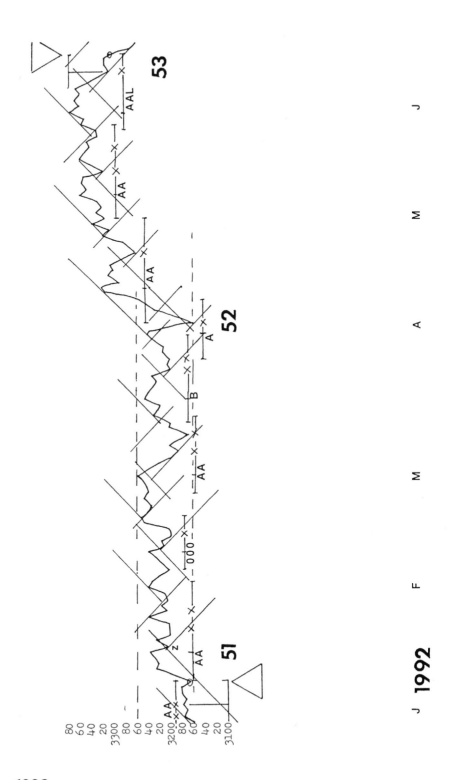

January–June 1992

54. The May/June sideways action was similar to what happened from January to April. An **E** line blocked any buy signal in the vicinity of 3360.

55. **AA** high broke through the **E** line but was quickly turned back. In September another **AA** signal came from a new low within the past four months at 3240.

56. Is this a *zigzag* in mid-October? Not really, because it did not hug the down-channel line when it retraced. Compare it to the one on September 1, and again, in mid-September. An **AA** came off a new low within the past four months.

57. After the *zigzag* came two little dips. It was decided to take the second dip and wait for the third with a *neutral* signal.

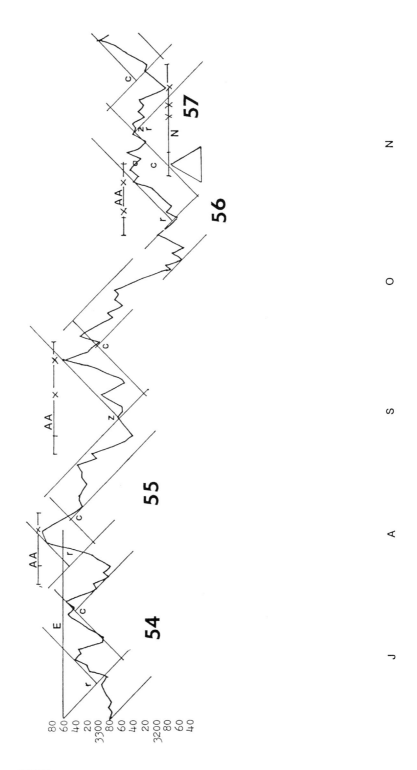

July–November 1992

58. In December an **NL** code was used because the price dropped through the last low in the up-channel and was balanced between 3360 and 3180.

59. The January sell signal was offset by the splendid support from the tops in October and November, as well as the low in mid-December. Place a *hold* at 3240.

60. A series of new highs prompted **AA** signals—until a triple top appeared, which caused no trouble. By mid-March four tops were lined up at about 3490. It finally was able to pierce the **E** barrier as shown in the following graph.

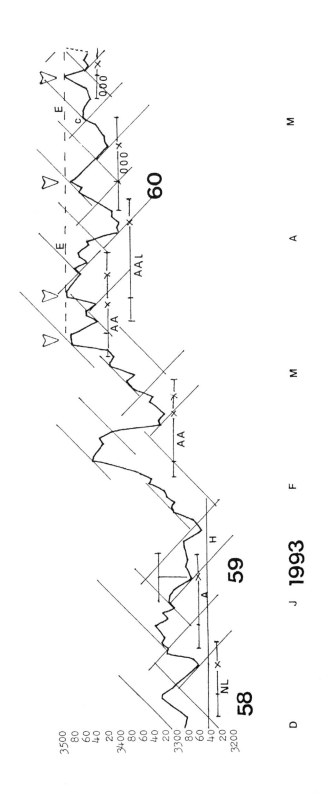

December 1992–May 1993

61. From a new all-time high came a drop that took out local support. A quick reverse from an **AAL** signal sparked a huge one-day rally. The code that followed could not be classified easily. Local support was taken out, but that support was weak. It might have been *neutral* or even an **NL**. A simple **AA** was decided upon.

62. A *neutral* **L** signal was suggested here, but a *hold* would have been equally acceptable.

63. The end of August brought an all-time high. When it dropped back to 3585, it could have been an **AAL**, having broken local resistance. The support beneath, however, was substantial; so an **AA** code was used. After the successful **B** signal, a *neutral* code used the first dip in the down-channel for measuring. It would have been better technique if the dip had been completely in the down-channel as at the second **X**.

Notice how the system skillfully side-stepped the various problem areas and avoided unnecessary sales for a whole year.

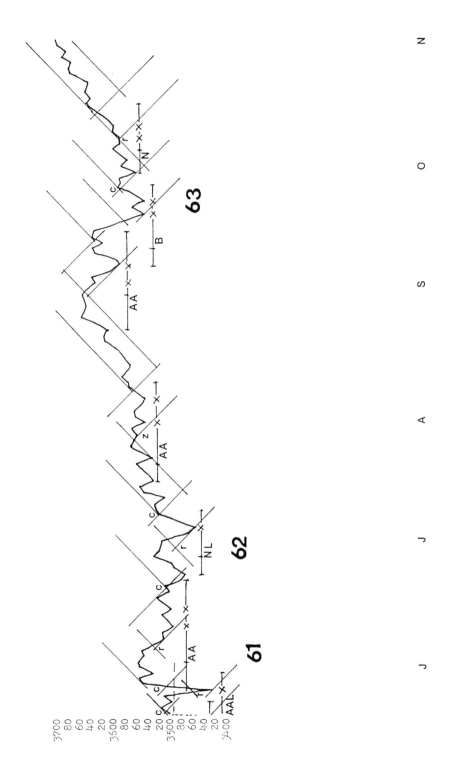

June–November 1993

64. The **A** signal fell way short of a new up-channel. The *"T"* fared even worse using the nearest top. By extending the *"T"* to the next top, the Dow had a chance to reach the up-channel. It is often suggested to split *target day* with the *"T"*. In this case, however, with such a nice run-up, and local support in tact, it seemed reasonable to allow the *"T"* to call the next move.

65. Here is the first sell signal since the purchase on November 1, 1992! An **AAL** label identified the breaking of local support in just one day. This was a serious break because there was no significant support for another 250 points.

66. The **AA** signal was called an **AA** low signal because there was no support within the past four months. Again, note the weird comparison with 1987. This time the first top in the up-channel, although not quite a *zigzag*, could possibly pass for one. The *"T"* *target day* managed to keep the Dow from severe damage.

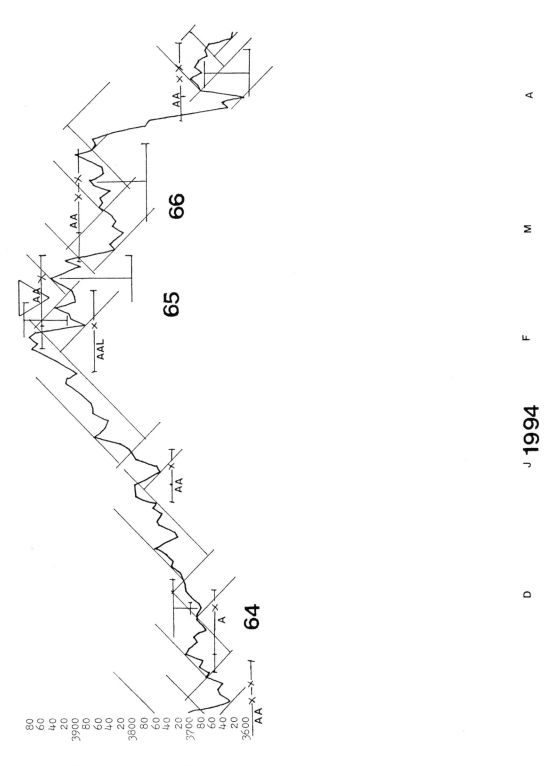

December 1993–April 1994

67. With what appeared to be a routine **B** signal, came a possible ***triple top*** once the up-channel was broken. The **B** signal was chosen because the upside potential was far greater. Support at 3600 called for a ***hold*** at that level, or at least a ***neutral***, rather than an **NL** code.

68. The price drop shattered all local support. Ordinarily you would want to sell at ***target day*** with an **AAL** signal, but three other lows within the past four months gave a strong triple bottom. Place a ***hold*** at 3600.

69. After the new all-time high at 3940, a precipitous drop in prices broke local support for a classical **AAL** signal.

    Actually, the sale should have been measured from the first top for only three days extension for an additional 25 points in profits.

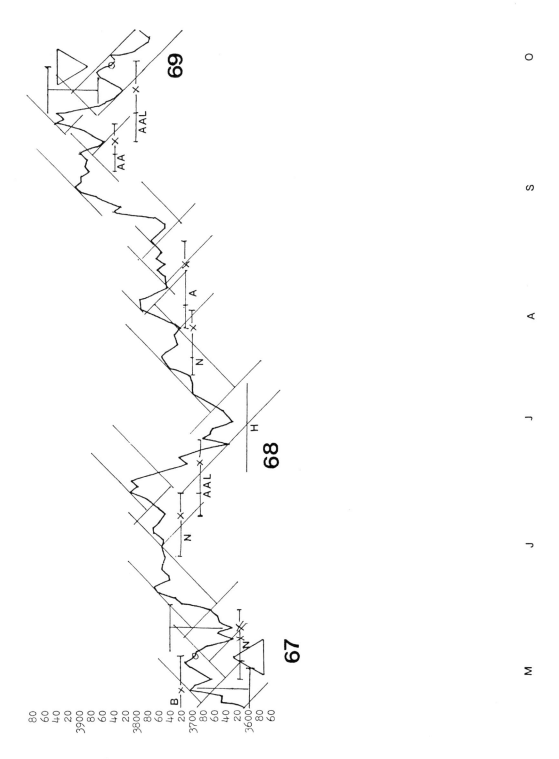

May–October 1994

70. A strong rally brought the Dow back to the 3940 area, which prompted an **E** blockade. A slight penetration of 3940 required an **AA** signal.

71. An **A** signal was used because of the important 3780 low in October.

72. December saw a new low within the past four months. Notice where the **XX** were placed. The second **X** was slightly higher than the first **X** and so the **"T"** signal was preferred. Place a *hold* at 3670.

73. At 3860 the price dropped into the down-channel for a *neutral* signal. Again, at the same price level, another *neutral* signal was used to bring about a strong *continuation* pattern.

74. With a new all-time high, an **AA** signal completed this study of the Dow Jones Industrial Averages.

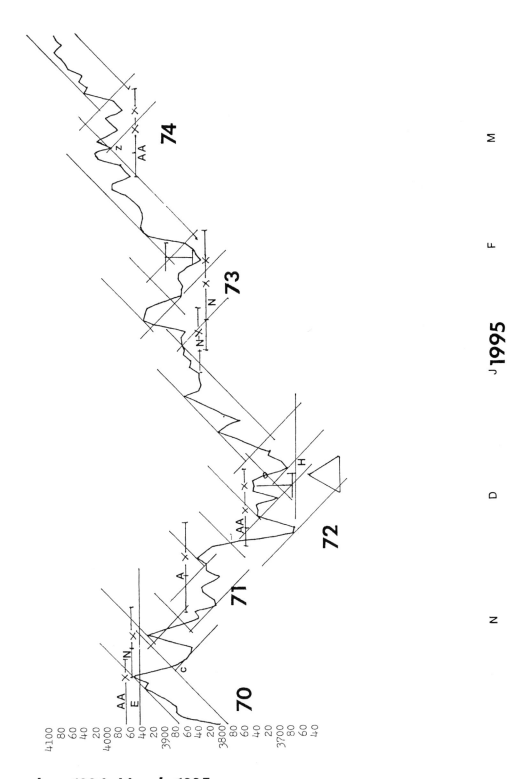

November 1994–March 1995

Update

In March of 1995, testing was concluded on the Dow Jones Industrial Average to confirm the value of the **PAMA Method**. We bring you this update for several important reasons:

1. There is a need to rescale the Dow and the S&P 500 because of the whopping 1600 point rise in the Dow since the conclusion of testing. The formula, 1600 ÷ 35 = 45.7, raises the scale of the Dow from 20 points to 50 points per large square.

2. The update provides an opportunity to compare the action of stocks to bonds in the same time period. By comparing the S&P 500 to the Benham Tg2000 (a zero coupon bond), you will see the wide divergence that is possible between the two. The lesson to be learned is that you cannot expect the S&P 500 to help call a signal for bonds . . . and vice versa.

3. When trading a stock or a bond fund, it is helpful to coordinate it with the proper index. Generally speaking, a stock or bond fund, with its diversification of issues, will mirror an index better than an individual stock or bond.

4. Finally, by reviewing the steps leading to a trade, it is hoped that you will gain a greater insight in the art of trading.

Benham Tg2000 and the Bond Fund of America

December 1995—Both charts had risen steadily since November and continued to rise into 1996. The Bond Fund of America showed a weak *zigzag*, but was not confirmed by the Benham chart. Note the use of the small **c** and **r** for labeling channel continuations and reversals.

January 1996—The upswing continued with the bond fund stronger than the Benham fund.

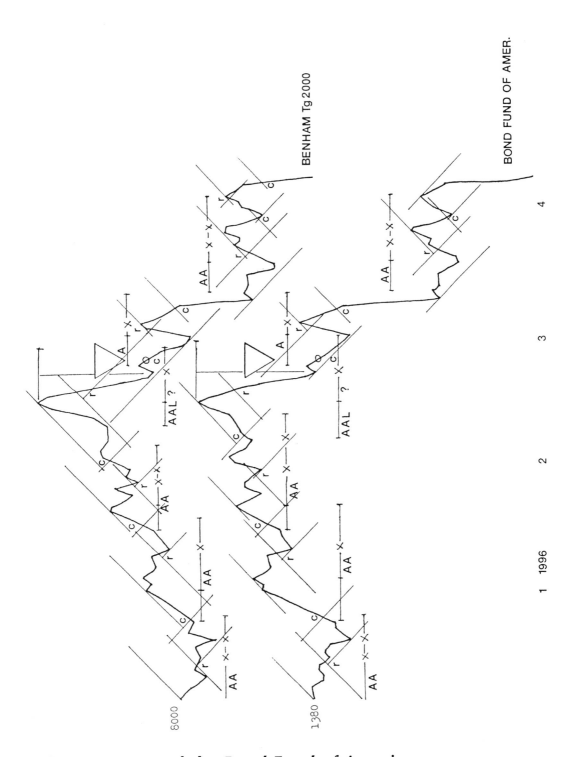

Benham Tg2000 and the Bond Fund of America

February 1996—At the end of January and the first of February, it was necessary to use both **XX** in order to clear the down-channel for the final run to the all-time new high on both charts. Suddenly, the big correction came, which called for deciding on what to do. It was pointed out on the checklist on page 149 that commodity future rules can be applied to any market. Since the Bond Fund of America was looking more like a commodity, it was decided to use the commodity runner signal (page 87) in place of the usual **AAL** signal.

March 1996—Because of the low last December, an **A** was used after the down-channel breakout, but a continuation pattern soon developed.

April 1996—On the first of the month, the Benham fund showed a brief foray into another up-channel, which did not hold while the bond fund stayed in the down-channel. How much farther down the fund will go remains to be seen. In any event, do not move too soon and try to outguess the system!

The S&P 500 and the American Mutual Fund

December 1995—Both charts had risen sharply since November in the same way that the bond fund had risen. The S&P 500 and the American Mutual fund both cleared the down-channel with the second **X** even though their prices were not quite synchronized.

January 1996—The American Mutual appeared to be much stronger than the S&P 500. An **A** was placed in position because of the low at the same price level in December. On the other hand, a **B** was appropriate for the S&P 500 because the price came down from an **AA** high, then up not exceeding the **AA** high, and then down again falling below the December low. Both signals cleared their down-channels.

February 1996—Unlike the bond fund and its index, the stock fund and the index did not collapse but rather went sideways. **B** signals cleared both charts.

March 1996—Finally, an **AAL** flashed a sell signal, which underscored the need to sell in view of the extreme weakness of the bond market. Could we expect it to follow the same path? Notice how the S&P 500 had dropped through two important support areas even more decisively than the American Mutual fund had dropped through its support areas. Notice how the *"T"* confirmed the signals. Place an **E** resistance line across the tops so there would be no temptation to buy just below it. By the end of March, American Mutual jumped into the up-channel and nearly penetrated the resistance line before turning down. The S&P 500 barely made it through to the up-channel before it also turned down, which was a red flag warning that there may be more weakness to come.

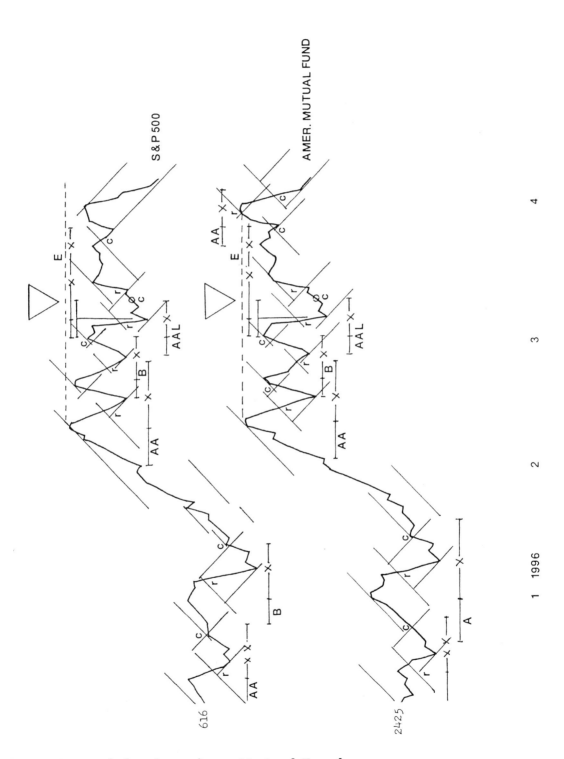

S&P 500 and the American Mutual Fund

Section III

Commodity Futures

◆◆◆◆

Applying the **PAMA Method** to Commodities

Although I started out trading the stock market, it didn't take long for the commodity futures markets to capture my attention. Like most traders, I was both drawn to, and initially scared off by, the high leverage inherent in futures. Legendary stories of multimillion dollar fortunes won—and lost—in a matter of weeks are commonplace in this most challenging of speculative arenas, simultaneously providing incentive to take part, and a reminder to do so cautiously. In fact, it was only after my confidence in **PAMA** was bolstered by stock market success that I finally opted to test the method with futures. Naturally, I was curious to see if my system would "cross over" to these higher reward/higher risk markets, and remain profitable.

Looking back now, venturing into commodities was probably the smartest thing I could have done, and it's where—today—I focus most of my trading energies. Having developed an extraordinarily proficient method for detecting market turn points, taking the natural next step into futures trading then allowed me to maximize return on **PAMA**'s unique ability.

That's not to say, though, that futures trading is for everyone. It's not. The stakes are higher, and the need for discipline greater. But if you "fit the profile," and you come equipped with an effective trading method, the potential for substantial profit is far greater with futures than it is anywhere else.

Applying the **PAMA Method** to futures was significantly easier than I expected it would be. **PAMA** proved both flexible and resilient, requiring only minor adjustments to make the transition. A short list of rule changes will be presented in this section. Each of the slight adjustments provided were necessitated by the fundamental, well-documented price behavioral differences between equities and futures.

Throughout this futures trading section, I again rely heavily on "walk-through" instructive examples, illustrating **PAMA** in action to train you in its use. I also touch briefly on commodity options, trading vehicles you may want to consider particularly if your risk capital is limited.

Rule Changes and Code Adjustments for Commodity Futures Trading

To use the **PAMA Method** with commodities, here are the handful of changes necessary:

- The **c** and **r** channel directions are dropped because futures use short trades.
- The **corner zigzag** rule does not apply to commodities.
- The **A** code is dropped and becomes the same as the **AA** code.
- The **AAL** code is dropped.

If you have access to commercial commodity charts, continue to divide 35 into the price range of a recent contract. For example, if the range from high to low is:

9–13 points, use 1/4 point per square

13–26 points, use 1/2 point per square

26–35 points, use 1 point per square

If a commodity is too volatile for its channel, cut the price scale in half, and if the commodity is not volatile enough, double the price scale. Without the aid of commercial charts, track an issue by testing the range. You will soon discover if it properly fits the channels.

Placing Stop Losses

Since losses must be kept at an absolute minimum, there will be more trading than with the Dow. Place stop orders on all long and short positions as follows:

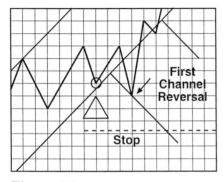

Place a stop four squares below the purchase price (see Figure 77). On the first channel reversal, and as prices hover near the purchase price, do not sell unless stopped out. After the equity leaves the *pivotal area*, this rule no longer applies.

Figure 77

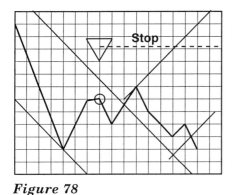

Figure 78

Short positions are treated the same way as long positions. Prices, under the protection of stops, can wander outside the channel (see Figure 78).

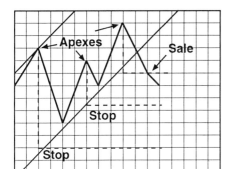

Figure 79

After prices have left the pivotal area to the up-side, do the following: Drop a vertical line from the apex to the lower up-channel line (see Figure 79). Place the stop where they intersect. Repeat until stopped out.

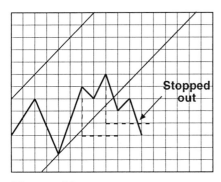

Figure 80

From the apex to the stop, there must be no less than four squares in between. This means that at times the stop will come *below* the channel intersection as shown in Figure 80.

The Runner Signal

After subtracting several signals from the Dow trading list, it will be necessary to add one important signal to the commodity trading list. This signal is called the **runner** because it rises or falls quickly and "runs" uninterrupted for just two or three days before retracing. Once underway, however, it can continue for quite some time in the same direction as the initial spurt. This signal can provide wonderful profits. The **runner** is important because often the Dow signals might not catch the trade at all. The rules that follow govern the **runner**. As always, what is true of long positions is equally true of short positions.

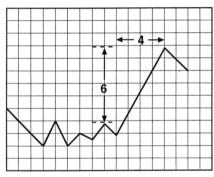

Figure 81

A ***runner*** consists of at least six squares of a noninterrupted price surge. Measurements for the six squares begin, not from the start of the surge, but rather from the last top nearest the surge. The surge can take from one to four days, but no more than four days (see Figure 81).

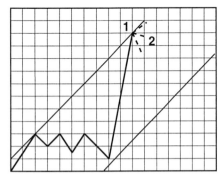

Figure 82

The end of the surge is marked with a **1**. The very next day is **interruption day (2)** where prices may go in a more or less sideways move—either up a little or down a little (see Figure 82).

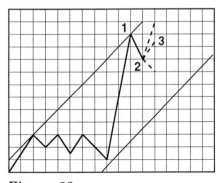

Figure 83

The third day is ***buy day*** (see Figure 83). It can be anywhere in the vicinity of point **1**—either above or below **1**. No fast rule can be made as to how far ***buy day*** can be from point **1**. It must, of course, remain in the up-channel.

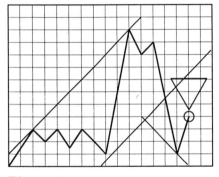

Figure 84

Figure 84 shows a situation where a ***runner*** faces a ***runner*** going in the opposite direction. This is a ***high-risk*** trade. It might call for rescaling your chart for less volatility.

This concludes the signals for trading commodities. A summary of all the commodity signals follows.

Buy/Sell Signals for Commodities

Channel Direction	Plan	Market Position	Extensions	Target Day (Minimum)
Up/Down	AA	New high/low in past four months	XX	3 days
Up	B	1) Up-channel from **AA** low	X	3 days
		2) Down-channel		
		3) Up-channel—Buy		
Down	B	1) Down-channel from **AA** high	X	3 days
		2) Up-channel		
		3) Down-channel—Sell short		
Up/Down	000	Triple top/bottom in past four months	X	2 days
Up/Down	N	*Neutral*—Buy/sell signal that comes between support/resistance	XX	3 days
Up	NL	Same as *neutral* except *last high* in down-channel has been penetrated on the first **X**	X	2 days
Down	NL	Same as *neutral* except *last low* in the up channel has been penetrated on the first **X**	X	2 days
Up	E	Disregard buy signals just below **E** because of strong resistance	*Do Not Buy*	
Down	H	Disregard sell short signals just above **H** because of strong resistance	*Do Not Sell Short*	
Up/Down	R	*Runner* (see page 87) for explanation		

As you can see, the rules for commodities match those of the Dow with the exception of adding the *runner* and eliminating the **A**, **AA** and *zigzag*.

> All signals are acted upon near the close of the trading day. Frequently, tops and bottoms are not labeled because *target day* and the *"T"* are obviously going to land outside the channel being measured.

It should be understood that the charts to follow are theoretical trades only. For a variety of reasons, the resulting profit/loss figures could be somewhat different from what has been recorded.

Commodities

S&P 500

June   During the first week of June a short *runner* was missed by just one-half a square; after which prices moved in and out of their channels so fast that no measurements were taken.

July   A *neutral* buy signal remained in effect until September.

October   An unusual whipsaw occurred when a *triple top* was quickly stopped only to be followed by a *runner* that was also stopped out.

5 Tick Min. = $25

1 Point = $500

Date	Buy	Date	Sell	Move	Profit / Loss	
7/16/93	446.95	9/8/93	456.65	970	$4,850	
10/14/93	465.95	10/12/93	461.95	400		$2,000
10/21/93	466.00	11/3/93	462.00	400		$2,000

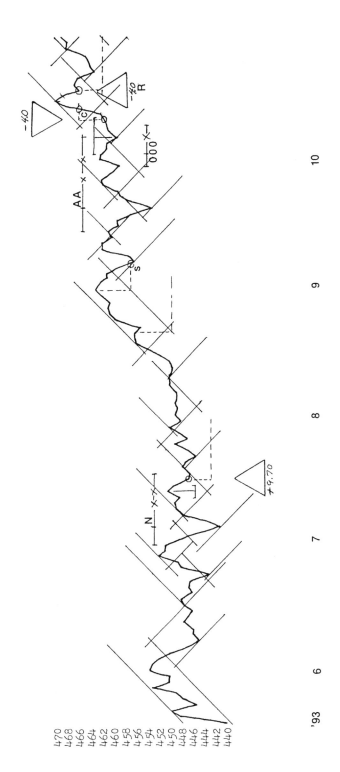

S&P 500

S&P 500

November   Resistance in the 453 to 459 area was too strong to risk shorting a *runner*. By mid-November a little double top at 467 allowed the use of the second **X** for measuring (see Figure 36). *Target day* left the up-channel. Because of the strong resistance at 458, a *neutral* short sale was used rather than an **NL**. It cleared the down-channel.

December   This **NL** is an aggressive signal to take, but notice the upward bias for the past five months. Back in September support from tops began at 462 as well as a base formed in the 458 area. It would seem, then, that an **NL** buy would have a better chance than a *neutral* shot had in November. A nice run was stopped out in February.

February   A normal *runner* was covered in March.

March   An **AA** long was saved by a *"T"*.

A short *runner* was considered, but *buy day* would come at 452, which was too far down from *interruption day*.

5 Tick Min. = $25

1 Point = $500

Date	Buy	Date	Sell	Move	Profit / Loss
12/10/93	463.90	2/4/94	474.00	1010	$5,050
3/7/94	467.10	2/8/94	471.90	480	$2,400

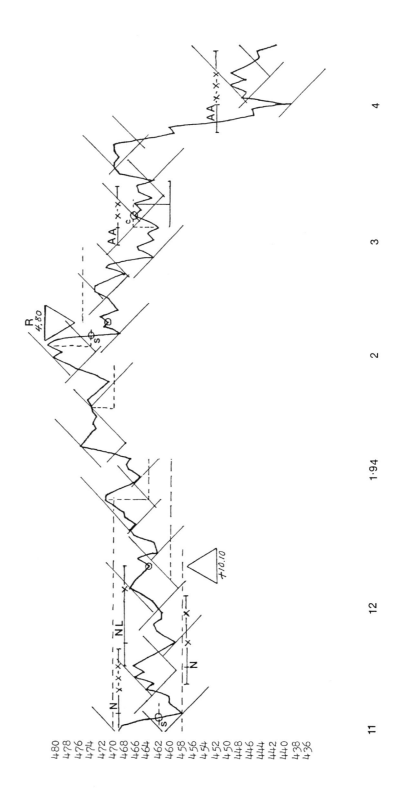

S&P 500

S&P 500

Note: Due to increased volatility, the scale has been cut in half.

April   The **AA** signal failure did not come as a surprise. More base building was necessary.

May   Another **AA** measurement landed right on the channel. It is best to wait one day.

June   This would be an **NL** signal except for the strong resistance at 464 in March.

July   A classic *triple bottom* stemming from April, May and June provided a strong base to launch a trade.

September   It was not until September that the trade was stopped out.

A **B** signal was shorted even though it faced stiff resistance a few points below.

5 Tick Min. = $25

1 Point = $500

Date	Buy	Date	Sell	Move	Profit / Loss
7/12/94	448.75	9/21/94	463.65	1490	$7,450
10/11/94	462.00	9/28/94	466.45	445	$2,225

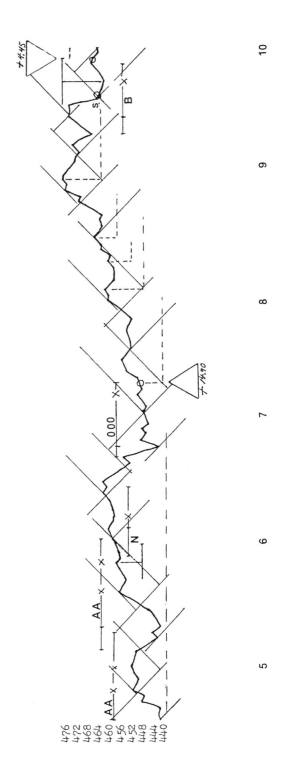

S&P 500

S&P 500

S&P 500

October   Because of strong resistance at 474–476, a *neutral* buy signal replaced an **NL**.

November This **NL** short is actually coming off a *triple top*, but by the time it was in a position to trade it had slipped into an **NL**.

December Note a mistake (on purpose). The stop on December 1 should have been extended to catch the price rising in the up-channel. Instead, a new stop was used, which lessened the profit by two points.

The lesson: Never raise a stop with a short position, and never lower a stop with a long position.

The **NL** buy could just as well have been an **AA**. The stunning results of 65 points in profits before being stopped out is a glowing tribute to the effectiveness of the system.

5 Tick Min. = $25

1 Point = $500

Date	Buy	Date	Sell	Move	Profit / Loss
12/16/94	461.80	11/9/94	465.80	400	$2,000
12/22/94	463.25	6/9/95	528.00	6474	$32,375

S&P 500

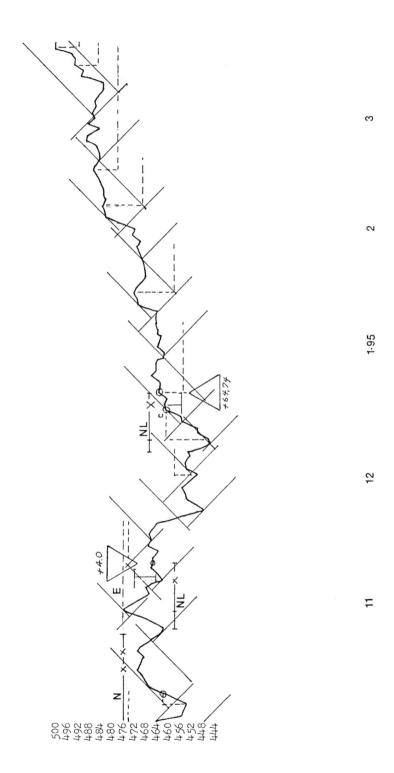

S&P 500

S&P 500

July   The S&P continued to climb after the sale. From a new all-time high came another opportunity to gain additional points with an **AA** code.

5 Tick Min. = $25

1 Point = $500

Date	Buy	Date	Sell	Move	Profit / Loss
6/29/95	548.45	7/19/95	556.00	775	$3,775

Summary for S&P 500

Profit	Loss	Net	No. Trades	% Profitable Trades
$60,125	$4,000	$56,125	10	80%

S&P 500

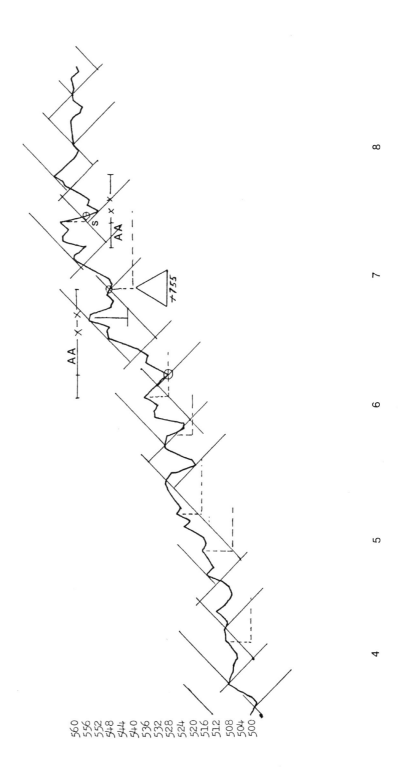

S&P 500

Pork Bellies

June	A *runner* without a history of support and resistance is a high-risk trade.
July	An **AA**, confirmed by a *"T"*, came out of a good base.
August	This **AA** short did not come from a good base; therefore, it would not be considered as safe as the trade in July.
	Take special note of the stop. A limit day up did not allow the short to be covered until 48. Therein lies the risk of futures trading!
September	The *runner* escaped being stopped out intraday in both September and October.
	Notice that, nine days after the *runner,* a stop would have resulted in a sale with no profit. Remember, the first pull-back after a signal is ignored and the original stop is retained.

Value $400 Per Cent

Date	Buy	Date	Sell	Move	Profit / Loss
7/2/93	36.00	6/1/93	38.80	2.80	$1,120
7/9/93	39.20	8/9/93	43.50	4.30	$1,720
8/25/93	48.00	8/16/93	43.35	4.65	$1,860
8/31/93	50.20	11/4/93	57.00	6.80	$2,720

PORK BELLIES

Pork Bellies

Pork Bellies

November   An **AA** short came out about even after commissions and possible slippage.

December   The **AA** buy is not easily classified. 51 is the low for the past three months—not four months.

An **NL** is too close to the base.

It was decided to go for the **AA**, but *target day* landed outside the up-channel. Observe the next attempt at 57. At first glance it looks like a perfect **NL**, but the rule says that the first **X** must be above the last high in the adjoining channel. Here, however, the last high is two channels away. A simple *neutral* signal was tried.

January   A *neutral* signal fizzled out a few days later for a loss.

A possible *runner* emerged at the end of the month, but an **E** at 61 prevented taking a position.

February   The **NL** boundaries were difficult to determine. Was the up-channel really violated? How should the *target* line be drawn? It was decided to forgo a trade.

March   Another **NL** was unable to remain in the up-channel.

April   **HV** was not evident until the second **X**.

Value $400 Per Cent

Date	Buy	Date	Sell	Move	Profit / Loss	
12/9/93	54.25	11/15/93	55.40	1.15	$460	
1/31/94	57.22	1/21/94	55.22	2.00		$800

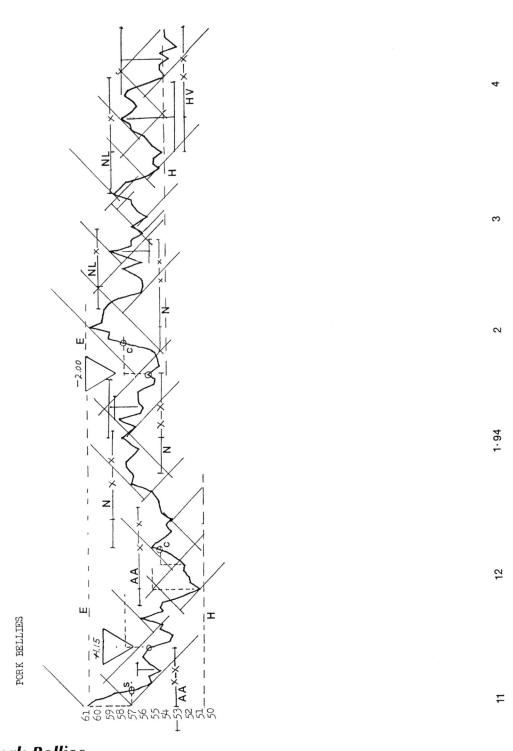

Pork Bellies

Pork Bellies

April   An **HV** supported by a *"T"* produced a splendid short trade.

June   A *runner* added another winner.

August   A *runner* from a single spike down is a high-risk trade since there is no base of support.

On August 25 the price went from 3155 to 4375. A gap of this magnitude is a warning not to attempt a *runner*. The price could gap down for a serious loss.

September By the middle of the month, prices stabilized enough to try a short **AA** trade.

Value $400 Per Cent

Date	Buy	Date	Sell	Move	Profit / Loss
6/6/94	42.00	4/11/94	53.50	11.50	$4,600
8/5/94	31.02	6/27/94	38.95	7.93	$3,172
8/10/94	33.47	8/18/94	31.47	2.00	$800
10/27/94	41.80	9/16/94	40.52	1.25	$500

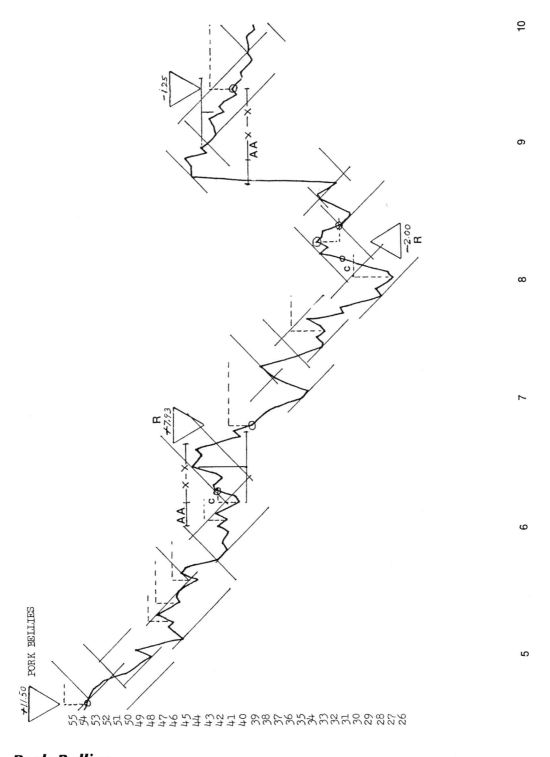

Pork Bellies

Pork Bellies

November   The **AA** short was covered in December at the same time a *neutral* buy signal was taken.

December   This trade was labeled a *neutral* because the price at 36 1/2 came roughly between 27 and 43. The first **X** of the *neutral* signal did go above the local resistance, but the formation was not convincing enough to call it an **NL**.

January   What seemed like a *runner* did not rise six squares above the adjacent top.

February   The **AA** short sale was not made because it looked like the down-channel would not hold. An **NL** buy signal followed.

Value $400 Per Cent

Date	Buy	Date	Sell	Move	Profit / Loss
12/12/94	36.67	11/14/94	41.35	4.68	$1,872
12/12/94	36.67	1/09/95	40.75	4.08	$1,632
3/01/95	43.15	3/23/95	45.20	2.05	$820

PORK BELLIES

Pork Bellies

Pork Bellies

March "A *runner* followed by a *runner* is going in the opposite direction in a high-risk trade."

April After dropping to a four-month low, an **AA** sell short signal was quickly covered.

May This is not a short *runner* since it has taken more than four days to form.

June Another **AA**, dropping into a new four-month low, did not stay in the down-channel. Prices, coming off a new low, catapulted upward to form a *triple top*. A brief new high prompted an **AA**, which also failed to hold in the up-channel. It was not worth trying for the *triple top* unless a position could be taken closer to the top of the price range.

July By the middle of the month, it was evident that a *triple bottom* had formed. Here again, it was not possible to enter close enough to the bottom of the price range. What about buying a *runner*? The whole formation has a slight upward bias starting last May. Even though a new high was reached, the upward bias would suggest that the top of the range had been met.

Value $400 Per Cent

Date	Buy	Date	Sell	Move	Profit / Loss
4/12/95	41.82	3/29/95	39.82	2.00	$800
5/12/95	38.50	4/28/95	39.47	.97	$388

Summary for Pork Bellies

Profit	Loss	Net	No. Trades	% Profitable Trades
$18,504	$4,760	+$13,744	15	67%

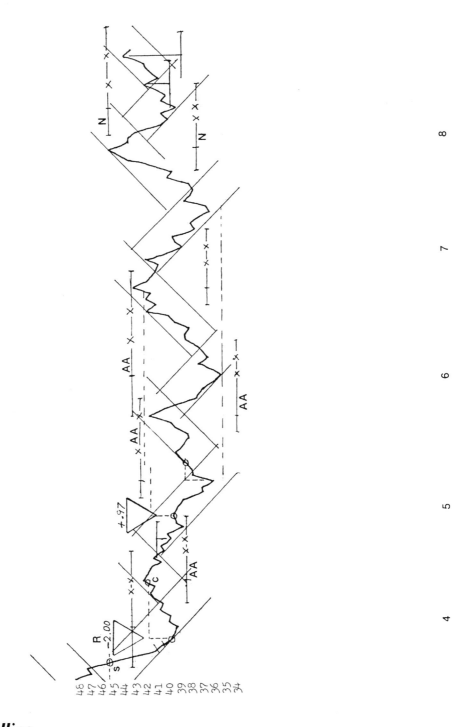

Pork Bellies

Silver

June   An **AA** buy signal was stopped out by an intraday low in July.

July   This could not be a *runner* because there are too many interruptions, and more than four days to form.

August   A powerful short *runner* was stopped in October.

October   A *runner*, weakened by a hesitation at 430, was strengthened by rising above local resistance. You might have been justified by going for an **AA** instead. The results would have been about the same.

Value $50 Per Cent

Date	Buy	Date	Sell	Move	Profit / Loss
6/30/93	456.00	7/22/93	485.00	29	$1,450
10/4/93	422.00	8/10/93	476.00	54	$2,700
10/6/93	429.00	11/29/93	450.00	21	$1,050

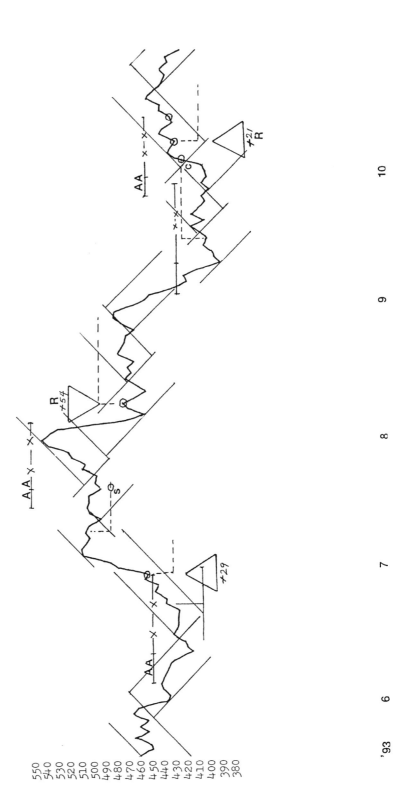

SILVER

Silver

Silver

December An **AA** buy signal was caught in a tight trading range.

It would have been better to let the original stop stay in place and sell in March.

February A *runner* went to a new high followed by a sale in March.

April Because of the exceptionally strong resistance in the 500–510 area, no short should be considered.

Value $50 Per Cent

Date	Buy	Date	Sell	Move	Profit / Loss
12/15/93	509.00	1/27/94	495.00	14	$700
2/7/94	524.00	4/5/94	554.00	30	$1,500

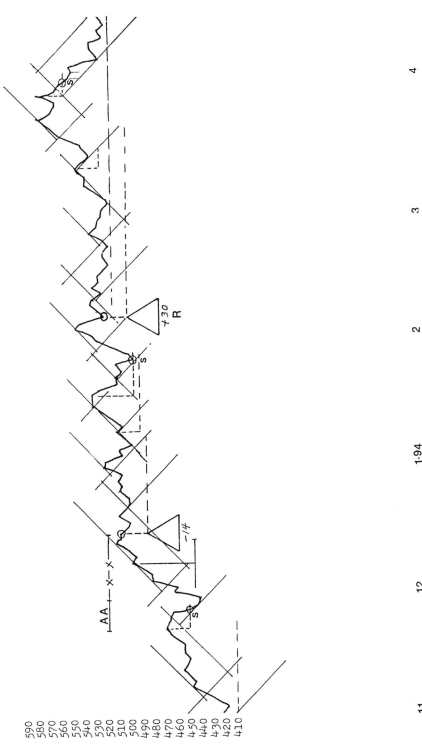

Silver

Silver

May   Strong support at 510 dates back to February for a 000 *triple bottom* signal.

As a *target day* arrived for the **AA** short attempt, prices dropped too close to the 510 resistance level for a decent profit. The *"T"*, however, took it out of the down-channel anyway.

June   A *neutral* signal rather than an **NL** was used because of the weak adjacent top.

July   After the **NL** signal, prices drifted lower for two months before being stopped out.

September An **NL** signal was stopped out with a minor loss.

Value $50 Per Cent

Date	Buy	Date	Sell	Move	Profit / Loss
5/4/94	517.00	6/1/94	535.00	18	$900
8/26/94	527.00	7/1/94	540.00	13	$650
9/6/94	547.00	10/13/94	544.00	3	$150

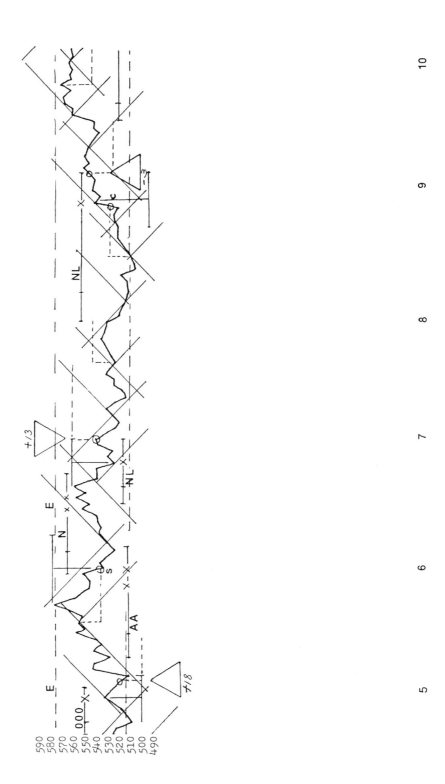

Silver

Silver

October   Another **NL** signal drifted lower for two months before being stopped out.

January   A **B** signal took a loss.

February   Why not take the ***triple bottom*** (December, January, February)? The answer is there is now resistance in December and January at 490. Furthermore, 510 in November is probably still exerting an influence. There simply is not enough room to maneuver for a decent profit.

March   A ***runner*** was missed by a half square.

An **AA** short used the third **X** for measuring, but did not stay in the down-channel.

Value $50 Per Cent

Date	Buy	Date	Sell	Move	Profit / Loss
12/28/94	485.00	10/18/94	538.00	53	$2,650
1/18/95	490.00	01/27/95	470.00	20	$1,000

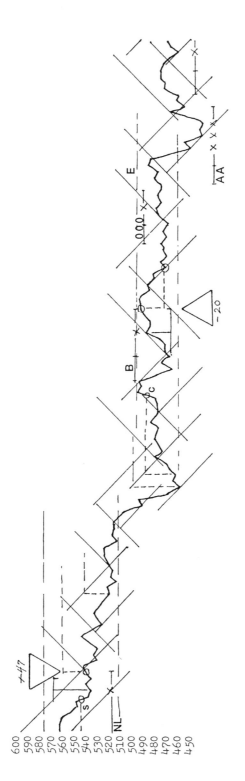

Silver

Silver

April   A *runner* rose above the 490 resistance level of the past four months. It was stopped out one month later.

May   Another *runner* provided a small profit.

July   An **AA** buy signal was sold at the end of the test run.

Value $50 Per Cent

Date	Buy	Date	Sell	Move	Profit / Loss
4/4/95	530.00	5/9/95	570.00	40	$2,000
5/17/95	530.00	5/15/95	541.00	11	$550
7/20/95	512.00	8/22/95	566.00	54	$2,700

Summary for Silver

Profit	Loss	Net	No. Trades	% Profitable Trades
$16,150	$1,850	$14,300	13	77%

Silver

Soybeans

June   A *runner* without a history of resistance in the area can be a risky trade. A strong *runner* developed into a powerful upward thrust.

July   Before a stop was put in place, it was decided to cut the volatility in half.

A short *runner* on the adjusted scale was taken.

The risk of this trade was somewhat lessened by the price dropping through local support.

September   An **AA** short brought a modest profit.

Value $50 Per Cent

Date	Buy	Date	Sell	Move	Profit / Loss
6/17/93	600.00	6/3/93	590.00	10	$500
6/24/93	626.00	7/27/93	705.00	79	$3,950
8/23/93	672.00	7/30/93	685.00	13	$650
11/3/93	630.00	9/15/93	640.00	10	$500

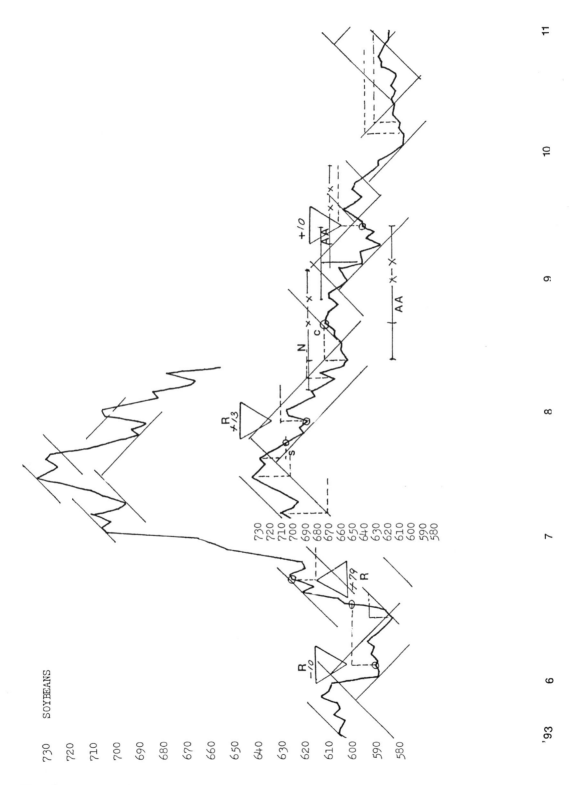

Soybeans

Soybeans

November   A *runner* was caught in a tight band for nearly three months.

February   Instead of waiting for the *runner* to be stopped out, it was covered at the same time that an **AA** short was taken.

Value $50 Per Cent

Date	Buy	Date	Sell	Move	Profit / Loss
11/12/93	675.00	2/2/94	683.00	8	$400
4/26/94	669.00	2/2/94	683.00	14	$700

Soybeans

Soybeans

May   An **AA** buy did not materialize, nor did a *neutral* short. This would not be a good *runner* to buy because of the slight interruption at 685. It might have been considered if it were not for the resistance at 710. The thrust to 730 was not quite six squares. An **AA** measurement took prices out of the up-channel.

July   A splendid short *runner* took out all resistance to the downside. An excellent trade.

August   On August 19, the price went to 6032 at the close. The high for the day was 6044, and the stop had been placed at 6050—a narrow escape!

Value $50 Per Cent

Date	Buy	Date	Sell	Move	Profit / Loss
11/15/94	560.00	7/7/94	624.00	36	$1,800

Soybeans

SOYBEANS

Soybeans

November   Because of the overhanging resistance in August at 570, this became a high-risk trade.

February   Prices remained dormant for so long that increased volatility seemed appropriate.

Value $50 Per Cent

Date	Buy	Date	Sell	Move	Profit / Loss
11/18/94	561.00	1/3/95	541.00	20	$1,000
2/9/95	554.00	4/13/95	575.00	21	$1,050

SOYBEANS

580
570
560
550
540

590
580
570
560
550
540
530

AA x—x

+21

AA x—x

−2o

c

s

11   12   1·95   2   3

Soybeans

Soybeans

June   Remember, a pair of *runners* facing each other going in opposite directions indicates a risky trade especially if the second *runner* faces resistance. Such was the case here.

By now, volatility was getting out of hand, and so it was cut in half.

Do not even consider an **NL** short sale because the last low in the up-channel was too insignificant. Even a *neutral* would have to land closer to 590 for a trade possibility.

July   The next signal started out as an **AA**, but because of the drop in price, a *neutral* signal was used. Serious resistance, however, prevented a short sale.

Value $50 Per Cent

Date	*Buy*	*Date*	*Sell*	*Move*	*Profit / Loss*
6/1/95	588.00	6/19/95	598.00	10	$500

Summary for Soybeans

Profit	*Loss*	*Net*	*No. Trades*	*% Profitable Trades*
$9,050	$2,000	$7,050	10	70%

Soybeans

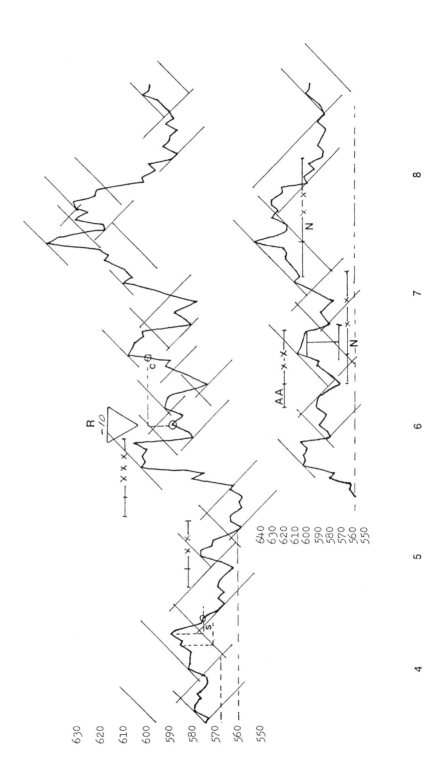

Swiss Franc

June   The first of the month brought a ***runner*** opposite a ***runner***, which is a dangerous trade. It was not attempted.

The **B** trade was rather risky in view of the drop already made.

August   The **AA** code has a special stop in this case: Notice the two well-formed bottoms at 65.25. The four-square stop would also fall at 65.25. To avoid a needless stop, it would be wise to drop the stop another two squares to 64.75.

September ***Target day*** and the **"T"** were two days apart, so split the difference for the trade day.

Value $1,250 Per Dollar Pt.

Date	Buy	Date	Sell	Move	Profit / Loss
8/2/93	66.85	6/21/93	66.31	.54	$675
8/9/93	66.46	9/21/93	70.50	4.04	$5,050
12/2/93	66.75	9/29/93	70.56	3.81	$4,762

Swiss Franc

Swiss Franc

December   You would have to look closely to catch the **B** signal. It might be argued that the low used in the down-channel was not the lowest low. With such a narrow band it would not make that much difference. This looked like an excellent opportunity to get aboard in view of the strong base in the 66–67 area dating back to July.

January   Prices slipped back to the base creating an even stronger base for the **NL** signal.

April   After the **AA** failed to provide a signal, prices dropped far enough to give an **NL** signal.

Value $1,250 Per Dollar Pt.

Date	Buy	Date	Sell	Move	Profit / Loss
12/2/93	66.75	12/29/93	68.12	1.37	$1,712
1/13/94	67.53	3/15/94	69.53	2.00	$2,500
4/28/94	70.08	4/12/94	69.08	1.00	$1,250

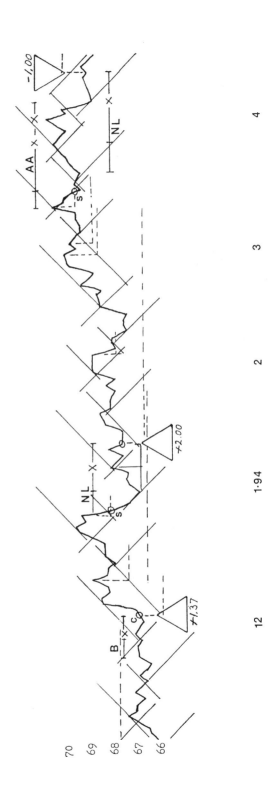

SWISS FRANC

Swiss Franc

Swiss Franc

May   Prices jumped through overhead resistance at 70 1/2; thus, an **AA** was attempted. The stop tripped it up the next day. If the second **X** had been used and not the third **X**, it might have missed the stop. A second **AA** was successful. This demonstrated how important it is to take every trade. You never know when the big one will come along!

July   This **AA** short leaves much to be desired. First, the Swiss Franc was in a highly bullish mode. Second, the price dropped from a single top, which offered little support. Finally, it was reversing at 74, which was a mild resistance area from last month.

August   An **AA** code was used here even though support was only three months ago, but very far below!

September An **AA** signal came as the price entered a slightly new high area. Any significant drop could constitute a *triple top* with an upward bias.

Value $1,250 Per Dollar Pt.

Date	Buy	Date	Sell	Move	Profit / Loss
5/9/94	70.89	5/10/94	69.89	1.00	$1,250
5/31/94	71.23	7/14/94	76.12	4.89	$6,112
8/1/94	75.30	7/26/94	74.30	1.00	$1,250
8/9/94	74.98	8/26/94	76.50	1.51	$1,887
9/20/94	77.89	10/28/94	79.50	1.61	$2,012

SWISS FRANC

Swiss Franc

Swiss Franc

November   This **AA** short was a bit safer than the one in July. The top was not a single spike as in July and the run-up not as dynamic. There was, however, considerable resistance at 78.

December   A *runner* popped out of a nice base.

February   Wedged between 75 and 80.75, an **NL** short looked promising, but was not to be. Then a *runner* made a terrific gain—so much so that it was decided to cut the volatility in half.

Value $1,250 Per Dollar Pt.

Date	Buy	Date	Sell	Move	Profit / Loss
12/28/94	76.25	11/11/94	78.07	1.82	$2,275
12/30/94	76.73	1/31/94	78.12	1.39	$1,737
2/14/95	78.42	2/03/95	77.42	1.00	$1,250
2/23/95	80.18	3/30/95	86.00	5.82	$7,275

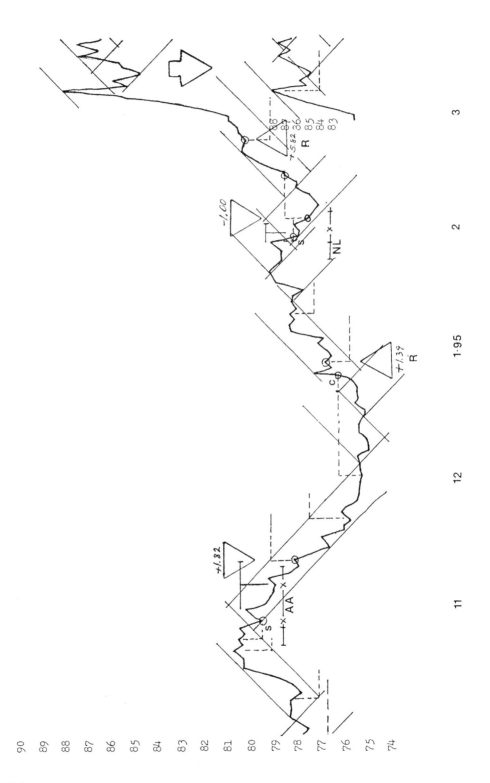

Swiss Franc

Swiss Franc

April   The **AA** buy attempt was bucking a double top. ***Target day*** narrowly exited the up-channel.

May   Even though the up-phase of the **B** signal was slightly above the first phase (April 1), it was close enough for our purposes.

Those who are new to this work might say it was just luck calling for a short position at this time, but those who have grasped the method know that it wasn't luck at all!

June   The ripple effect during the first half of June provided no opportunity for measurements. An **E** was placed at 89 1/2 to warn of strong resistance.

July   The first of the month, a ***neutral*** signal provided another excellent short.

Value $1,250 Per Dollar Pt.

Date	Buy	Date	Sell	Move	Profit / Loss
5/25/95	85.00	5/3/95	88.54	3.54	$4,425
8/22/95	81.29	7/6/95	87.97	6.68	$8,350

Summary for Swiss Franc

Profit	Loss	Net	No. Trades	% Profitable Trades
$48,097	$5,675	$42,422	17	71%

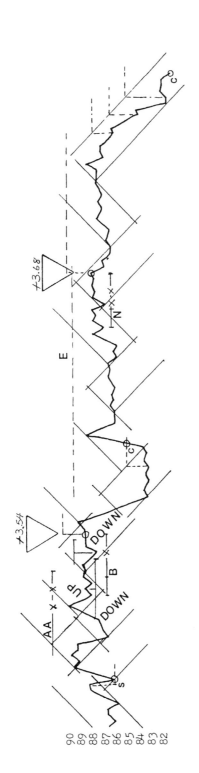

Swiss Franc

Options

*O**ptions,*** as related to commodities, open a new dimension for traders who cannot afford a straight commodity contract, or do not wish to take the risks associated with it. A full explanation of options is outside the scope of this book, but a brief description of their possibilities might encourage you to investigate further. The following chart demonstrates the dramatic rewards that are possible with a straight future contract, as well as the devastating risks. Finally, it will be shown how to trade options having complete control over the amount of money you wish to risk.

Coffee

March–April	Prices did little more than mark time. There was no incentive to buy long or sell short.
May	Was there a sudden shortage of coffee that summer? Before it became obvious that something was happening, a perfect *runner* got us aboard.
June	If, at the end of June, you had shorted coffee at the channel break (heaven forbid), you would not have been able to cover your position until about 195. Since coffee's value is $375 per cent, you would have lost $24,375 on one contract in just a week! On the other hand, our *runner* profit would have been a towering $45,750!

Before you throw up your hands at the thought of such large loss possibilities, turn to "Always Consider Options" to see how you can control these risks.

Value 1¢ Move = $375

Date	*Buy*	*Date*	*Sell*	*Move*	*Profit / Loss*
5/94	108.00	7/94	230.00	122	$45,750

*****Limit Days**—You can neither buy nor short. Trading resumes when a solid line appears.

Coffee

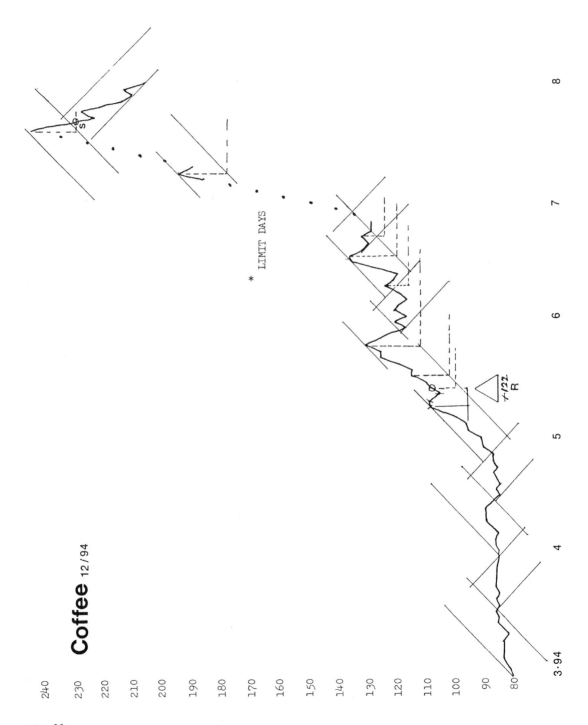

Coffee 12/94

* LIMIT DAYS

Always Consider Options

Briefly, here are the basics for understanding options.

Call Option. If you think a commodity is going up, buy a call option.

Put Option. If you think a commodity is going down, buy a put option.

Strike Price. *The Wall Street Journal* lists all the call options at the various price levels called the Strike Price. Look for August on the Pork Bellies chart (on page 145). Notice the figures above the **AA** purchase price. They represent how much it might cost to buy a call at the various price levels. For example, the strike price at 44 would be about $1,320 while the strike price at 56 would be only $165. Why? Because the closer you are to the strike price, the more expensive it becomes. The catch is, you can only make a profit if the price goes above the strike price.

Time. Time is the enemy of options because each option has an expiration date. When the option expires, and the price remains below the strike price, you will lose the cost of the option. The shorter the expiration date, the cheaper the cost of the option. The farther out, the more expensive it becomes. Example: Suppose you bought an option at the strike price of 50. It might cost about $508. If the option expired on October 1, you would lose $508. If the option, on the other hand, expired in December you would pocket about $3,200 minus $508 and commissions.

Puts. These options are the opposite of call options. If you think a certain commodity is going down, then you would buy a put. You would make a profit provided the commodity went down past the strike price at the expiration date.

One drawback to trading options is that there can be no stops to catch a market going against you. It will be necessary to call your broker near the close of the trading day, especially if the price is approaching a stop you have set on your chart.

Pork Bellies

In August the **AA** signal was stopped out near the end of September. What would be your profit if you had bought the contract? From the purchase price of 43 to the sale price of 48 is 5 cents. Pork bellies cost $400 per cent, which is 5 × $400 = $2,000 profit.

In October a short was purchased at 47 1/2, but was stopped out at 49 1/2 for a 2 cent loss of $800.

From there you might have bought pork bellies again at 52 in October and sold it at 57 (57 − 52 = 5). 5 × 400 = $2,000. Adding it all up: $2,000 − $800 + $2,000 = $3,200.

Let's consider buying an option instead of a future contract. At the strike price of 44, it would cost around $1,320 for a three-month option. If you sold it at the sell signal in October, you would realize a profit of $1,600 minus the cost of the option, or $280. But some premium would be left to add to the profit.

Supposing you decided to risk the small profit by retaining the option for the full three months to November. Now you would have 16 × 400 = $6,400 minus the cost of the option for a final profit of $5,080.

Say you could only afford to pay $165 for an option. For even less money, you could buy a two-month call option. By trying to save money, you would have lost the entire deposit because the price of pork bellies never reached 56. Let's say that you bought a three-month call option instead. Naturally, you would not have sold it in October, but waited for expiration in November. The price went to 60. The profit lies at whatever is above the strike price of 56 which is 4, and so 4 × 400 = $1,600 less the deposit of $165, which is $1,435. Not a bad profit in three months!

Do not trade with money you cannot afford to lose. Start with cheaper options, and as your profits mount, buy more than one option or buy closer to the strike price. There are many other strategies not mentioned in this brief account that you might want to investigate.

Pork Bellies

August   An **AA** signal brought a nice profit at the end of September.

October   A short was covered for a loss four days later.

Another **AA** was stopped out in a pivotal area for a good profit.

December In exactly six squares down a *runner* was covered in January.

Value 1¢ Move = $400

Date	Buy	Date	Sell	Move	Profit / Loss	
8/89	43.00	9/89	48.50	+5.50	$2,200	
10/89	49.50	10/89(s)	47.50	−2.00		$800
10/89	52.00	12/89	58.50	+6.50	$2,600	
					————	
					$4,800	$800

Pork Bellies

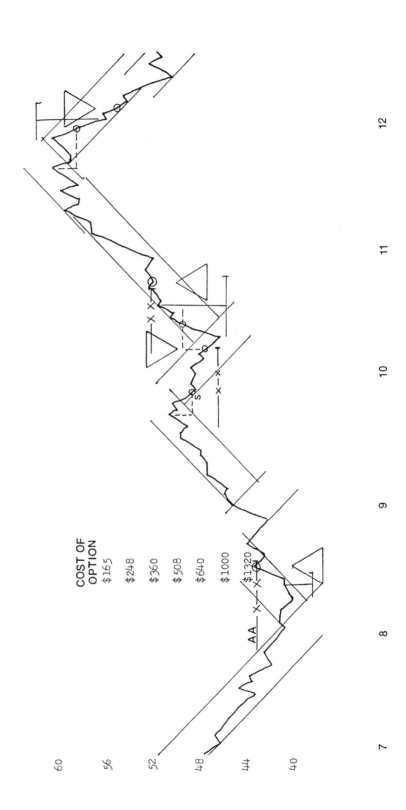

PORK BELLIES 7/90

COST OF
OPTION

$165

$248

$360

$508

$640

$1000

$1320

Summary of Options vs. Commodity Contracts

Option Advantage. All possible losses are predetermined.

Contracts. Losses can be unlimited, even with a stop loss.

Option Advantage. Buying an option costs only the price of the option plus commission.

Contracts. To open an account can cost several thousands of dollars depending on the contract.

Option Advantage. Options are much less risky.

Contracts. Commodity contracts expose you to greater risks.

Option Disadvantage. No stop loss protection.

Contract. Stop loss protection.

Option Disadvantage. Profits are possible only above a call's strike price, or below a put's strike price.

Option Disadvantage. Time, below the strike price of a call, can erode the value of a call to zero. Likewise, time can erode a put to zero above the strike price.

For the Beginner

If you are a novice, you should limit your commodity trading to options until you have become highly knowledgeable and have made a profit with options.

Note: It is true that there is protection for contracts with the use of stop losses, and many small losses occur at the purchase-stop area. One advantage of options over contracts is *not* using stops. Many of these small losses turn into profits by ignoring the initial reversals.

A Final Word

Before making a decision to buy or sell, it might be wise to review the following checklist:

1. Does **target day** fall within a reasonable number of days for the market to deliver a **continuation** pattern?

2. How well does the **target day** line up with the **"T"**, and which one looks more valid?

3. Is there **support** or **resistance** to consider? Look back four months.

4. Am I being unduly influenced by the media?

5. Am I afraid to buy in an up-channel when the market is falling that day, or sell in a down-channel when the market is going up that day?

6. Statistically, there is a greater chance of a **continuation** pattern than a **reversal** pattern.

7. Make sure you trade the system and not the emotions.

8. No matter what you are trading, if you need to limit losses as much as possible, trade by the commodity rules.

If you have any questions concerning the system, write. We will try to answer all questions. It will not be possible, however, to advise on any particular trade, nor can the author or publisher be liable for any loss resulting from following the **PAMA Method** rules.

For ease of maintaining your charts, the following aids can be sent to you: a plastic guide for drawing in the channels (a great time saver) and a sample chart with squares compatible with the plastic guide. The chart paper can be copied. Please include $3 for shipping and handling.

Jeffrey A. Cuddy
1039 Chestnut St.
Manchester, NH 03104

About the Author

Jeffrey Cuddy received his art education in Cleveland, Ohio, before entering the Air Corp during World War II, where he instructed pilots and navigators under the direction of Barry Goldwater.

After the war, Mr. Cuddy became the art director for WMUR-TV in Manchester, New Hampshire, after which he became president of Interstate Advertising, Inc. He was assistant to Bob Montana, creator of the famous comic strip, "Archie," until Mr. Montana's death in 1975.

For the past 20 years, Mr. Cuddy researched the stock market from a technical point of view. Unwilling to settle for current popular theories, he has developed new and exciting methods of charting. The work he has done has brought new insights into the field of market timing for both the stock market and the commodity futures market.

Jeff Cuddy and his wife Min have two children and two grandchildren.

Index